One Lone Courageous Doctor

Curing Strangled Voices (SD)
Spasmodic Dysphonia

vs

𝕿𝖍𝖊 𝕹𝖊𝖜 𝖄𝖔𝖗𝖐 𝕿𝖎𝖒𝖊𝖘 and
The Entire Medical Establishment
Guaranteeing No Cures

Part 2

The Medical Mystery Solved by a Doctor's Natural Voice Treatment:
Direct Voice Rehabilitation

F.D.A. Orders Warning Label for Botox and Rivals

Dr. Morton Cooper

Voice & Speech Company of America   Los Angeles

Introduction

"All the News That's Fit to Print." It's a wonderful slogan, and has graced page one of *The New York Times* ever since the late Nineteenth Century. In the days of New York's newspaper wars and the resulting rise of yellow journalism, the slogan meant that *The Times* would not play up sordid stories of lust and murder, would not cater to the prurient interests of people. The New York City described in the pages of *The Times* was often quite different from the New York City chronicled by the tabloids. For good reason the paper became known as the Gray Lady of Times Square.

But, as *The Times* evolved into not just the dominant paper in the New York metropolitan area but also America's newspaper of record, the slogan came to suggest that one of the paper's goals is to print comprehensive and balanced reports on all important topics of general interest. I think most journalism experts would agree with me on two points. First, as a practical matter it is impossible for any single newspaper, even one with the lofty ideals and substantial resources of *The Times*, to achieve this goal. Second, nonetheless *The Times* has come closer to this goal than any other newspaper in the country, and for this deserves the admiration of its competitors and the gratitude of its readers.

However, as we will see, sometimes all the news that's fit to print doesn't get printed, and that fact was one of the reasons I wrote this book. Back on March 11, 1992, *The Times* ran a column by Jane E. Brody, the paper's highly esteemed (and rightly so) health reporter. In that column she wrote that the only effective treatments for spasmodic dysphonia (SD) — "strangled voice" — are surgery or Botox injections. While it is true that many surgeons and physicians at the time maintained this view — after all, they were the people doing the surgery or giving the Botox injections — the fact is that there are no documented cases of either medical therapy or a single cure ever. However, there are many documented cases of an entirely different approach resulting in permanent cures by my different approach called Direct Voice Rehabilitation (DVR). I developed DVR (forty-five years ago) when I was associated with the Medical Center at the University of

California, Los Angeles. Later, in 1973, I published a textbook, *Modern Techniques of Voice Rehabilitation*, that described my cure for spasmodic dysphonia.

In 1980, I reported a series of documented cures of SD in the prestigious *International Association of Logopedics and Phoniatry* (IALP). The report was peer-reviewed. I also followed up SD cases I referred to Dr. Dedo, the surgeon for SD to realize the negative surgery outcomes in all too many cases. In 1994, the American Speech- Language and Hearing Association (ASHA) wrote that 2/3's of those doing that surgery were 2/3's worse off than before. I had also reported cures of SD at ASHA conventions in 1974, 1979, 1980, and 2000.

It's understandable, then, why I was disturbed that Ms. Brody's column omitted any mention at all of the cures I had achieved. After all, *The Times* is read in disproportionate numbers by physicians and other healthcare professionals, who were being told that two treatments for spasmodic dysphonia were effective when, in fact, I knew they were not. Moreover, the one treatment that was curative was omitted from her report.

Well, thought I, a succinct but fact-filled letter to the editor would result in a follow-up column about Direct Voice Rehabilitation. So within a few days I sent it off, along with a copy of *Modern Techniques of Voice Rehabilitation* and a printout of my peer-reviewed paper published in 1980 in *The Proceedings of the 18th Congress of the International Association of Logopedics & Phoniatrics*, in which I described cures for SD. I also cited my two consumer-oriented books (*Change Your Voice, Change Your Life* and *Winning with Your Voice*). I provided the names of the ENT doctors and the SD patients cured of SD to Ms. Brody. A simple phone call would lead Ms. Brody to other sources, and she would have a second column that would correct the dangerous misconceptions about surgery and Botox injections, and document that effectiveness of Direct Voice Rehabilitation.

It was not to be. Over the next dozen years I pursued the matter in a series of letters to *The Times* — to not only Ms. Brody but the editor, publisher and several others — all to no avail. The few responses I received were polite but vague, saying only that when the paper next writes about the subject it will keep me in mind.

Meanwhile, some important developments have occurred with respect to both surgery and Botox. According to the editor of the *Journal of Voice*, Robert Sataloff, M.D., the surgical procedure that Ms. Brody wrote about in her column has been relegated to the dustbin of medical history. As for Botox — it sounds like it could describe a cuddly stuffed animal or a tasty candy but it's the trademarked name for botulinum toxin (Bo for botulinum, tox for toxin), which is the world's most deadly poison. The physician who was Ms. Brody's source of information later joined the maker of Botox, Allergan Inc., as a top executive.

I am not surprised that the surgery pioneered by Dr. Herbert Dedo has all but disappeared as a treatment for spasmodic dysphonia. Unfortunately, in its place another surgical procedure has emerged, one that has left some spasmodic dysphonia patients with a permanently impaired voice or even no voice at all. I will not be surprised when Botox injections are discarded, although the economic argument in their favor are substantial: four to ten treatments or more a year at up to $4,000 each — for each and every year after year . . . for life! The simple fact is this: spasmodic dysphonia is not caused by a neurological affliction, so cutting or deadening nerves by surgery or toxic injections will not cure the problem. Medicine has not and does not report a single cure of SD ever. SD is not a result of acid reflux, allergies, or infections, as is medically believed. Nor is it a psychological problem; there are no reported cures in the annals of psychiatry since the syndrome was first identified more than one hundred and thirty-five years ago, in 1871 by Traube, who called it "nervous hoarseness," which became known as spastic or spasmodic dysphonia (SD) in today's medical terminology.

I have found that spasmodic dysphonia is due to the misuse of the voice, not by any neurological or medical condition. I have also clinically determined that SD develops psychological undertones because of the severity of the disorder itself but is not caused by per se psychological issues.

DVR is the only approach in the world that reports cures of SD. Please bear in mind that there cannot be cures unless causes are known, and I believe I have persuasively demonstrated that I have correctly identified the root cause. DVR essentially requires a month of intensive therapy and follow up sessions. It's not easy, but it can work and does work. [See testimonials at www.voice-doctor.com]

Over the years I have achieved a very high success rate with people suffering from impaired voices. These recoveries included many people who earn their living with their voices, including clergymen, entertainers, teachers and sales people. Take, for example, the experience of Ronald, a high-ranking executive with Herbalife. He was diagnosed and treated for his Spasmodic Dysphonia at the Mayo Clinic for one and one-half years, taking five Botox shots, without success. Finally, on the brink of losing his job because of his SD, he told his doctor at Mayo that he was terminating treatment there. The doctor spun through his Rolodex file cards, stopped at my name, and said, "Go see Dr. Morton Cooper." After Direct Voice Rehabilitation Ron was cured of his SD.

Consider also these testimonials, all from people suffering from S.D.

Schoolteacher

Just wanted to let you know how well my voice is holding up in my classroom, in restaurants, on the telephone, in cars, noisy places, and at home with my husband. I knew you could perform miracles when you cured my laryngitis (polyps) in three months by Direct Voice Rehabilitation when I first came to you in 1970, referred by my ear-nose-throat doctor, who has since retired.

When I couldn't find you in April 1985, during the onset of my spasmodic dsyphonia, I went to another ear-nosed-throat doctor. When I asked him where you were, he answered, "Oh, he's around." But he did not offer me your phone number. He treated me with antibiotics and referred me to his voice therapist, who told me that many people with spasmodic dysphonia get discouraged and go in for surgery. That really scared me.

Fortunately for me, I did find you and will be forever grateful to you for your expertise in curing my spasmodic dysphonia. Now, I am back teaching again, and I am delighted.

Zelda

Another cure:

My voice continues to be strong and firm, after nearly twenty years! It seems almost like a dream, those nine long years of strangled speaking. I'm so glad they're behind me.

I hope others continue to discover you and get the help they need. I hear from various spastic dysphonics from around the country and direct them to you. Whether they follow through or not, I don't know. For their sake, I hope they do!

A simple case of the flu set off a condition that became an extremely life-altering situation. What seemed like simple laryngitis just did not go away. I was seen by nine doctors, took speech therapy, was put on a limited diet, given two antibiotics, three allergy medications, a stomach medication, an antidepressant, various inhalers, and Prednisone, but nothing had any lasting effect.

Finally, I went to see two doctors at the UCLA Medical Center. They decided I had spasmodic dysphonia. One said my SD was different from most because both the abductor and adductor muscles were affected. He referred me to Dr. Morton Cooper. The simplicity of his treatment is the hardest part to believe, especially since there is supposed to be no cure for SD.

Now, fourteen years later, my voice remains excellent. I truly thank the Lord for Dr. Cooper and would recommend him to anyone who might have spasmodic dsyphonia.

Gayle Pace

Because of laryngitis and vocal misuse, my vocal chords gradually became weak in such a way that I could hardly speak. I consulted a cousin who, as a medical pathologist, was doing research at Rutgers. She said that I should first see Dr. F. and, if his treatment was not effective, to go to Los Angeles to see Dr. L.

I went to see Dr. L. who diagnosed my problem as spastic dysphonia and after extensive examinations referred me to Dr. Morton Cooper. I saw Dr. Cooper twice a week and, after a few months, regained my natural voice and also my career —

thanks to Dr. Cooper and his rehabilitation program.

University Professor

When I was being critiqued after some scene work, I mentioned that I was having trouble with my voice. One of the students recommended that I see Dr. Morton Cooper. Dr. Cooper told me that my voice was coming from the throat and that I was using shallow breathing. He simply taught me how to breathe from the diaphragm and to raise my voice up into the face mask area.

I later attended the Royal Academy of Dramatic Art in London, where I was again taught this very same method. Personally, I think it is criminal to offer an operation as an alternative to this straightforward treatment for spastic dysphonia. In Dr. Cooper's office I met several people who had this operation and they were absolutely no better for it.

Dr. Cooper is practicing vocal rehabilitation in a very effective way. His treatment works, and can be backed up by any legitimate voice coach.

Lisa

With documented results such as these, I will leave it to others to discern a motive for the medical community's indifference, and often outright opposition, to Direct Vocal Rehabilitation. But common sense tells us that any non-invasive therapy with a record of success is far preferable to unproved methods that involve either a sharp knife or a deadly poison.

Morton Cooper, Ph.D.

F.D.A. Orders Warning Label for Botox and Rivals

By Natasha Singer

May 1, 2009, *New York Times*, Business Section, Page B2, excerpts.

Botox and other similar anti-wrinkle drugs must now carry the most stringent kind of warning label, the Food and Drug Administration said Thursday.

The F.D.A. issued that order the day after the agency approved a new drug, Dysport, that is expected to be the first real challenger to Botox in the United States. Like Botox, Dysport is an injectable drug derived from the paralytic agent botulinum toxin.

The F.D.A. said such drugs must carry warning labels explaining that the material has the potential to spread from the injection site to distant parts of the body — with the risk of serious difficulties, like problems with swallowing or breathing.

Requiring a drug to carry a box with bold-face risk information — is one of the stronger safety actions the F.D.A. can take. Black boxes are typically reserved for medications known to have serious or life-threatening risks. Antidepressants, for example, carry black boxes warning of the increased danger of suicidal thought and actions.

The F.D.A. said it would also require makers of injectable toxins to send doctors letters warning of their risks and to produce a medication guide to be given to patients at the time of injection.

So Botox Isn't Just Skin Deep

By Natasha Singer

April 12, 2009, *New York Times*, Business Section, Page 1 & 10, (excerpt from page 10)

Of treating Stuttering with Botox, Dr. Mitchell Brin, the Vice-President of Development for Allergan the Botox drug maker says, "Stuttering is too complicated… it didn't pan out."

The Voice and Research Foundation

"I'm a fan of your work, and I've heard great things about you."
Roger Ailes
Chairman & CEO Fox News Network
says of Dr. Morton Cooper

Dear Colleague:

As you may be aware, I have demonstrated for many years that my exclusive non-invasive technique called Direct Voice Rehabilitation (DVR) can achieve dramatic results with spasmodic dysphonia (SD). This includes not only improvement or recovery but also cures. I'm writing to bring these results to your attention in the hope that you may find this information useful in your own practice as an alternative to invasive approaches.

Current medical treatment for spasmodic dysphonia focuses on two invasive options: Botox injections or surgery. The research literature has reported mixed results with surgery, and concerns about long-term use of Botox are increasing. Mitchell S. Brin, M.D., one of the pioneers in the use of Botox for SD, suggested at a conference on SD in March 1991 that this treatment should be withdrawn at the earliest possible time in favor of another substance. Serious negative side effects following the use of Botox have been reported by patients. Gerald Berke, M.D., chairman of the UCLA Head and Neck Division, commented in the December 1999 newsletter of the National Spasmodic Dysphonia Association that there are a number of "obvious drawbacks" to Botox: "It requires lifelong visits from 4 to 10 times per year for repeat injections. The injections are not inexpensive. The interval between post injection breathiness, good voice, and the return of symptoms may not be very long in some patients. Hypersensitivity and antibody formation have been shown to produce some long term structural changes in muscle cells."

Direct Voice Rehabilitation, by contrast, causes no harm. It combines proven techniques of voice rehabilitation in a new way that, with committed patients, produces lasting cures. The results I have achieved have been with patients diagnosed with SD by many of the leading laryngologists in the country. Many of my patients over the years have been diagnosed with SD by laryngologists who are listed below at the UCLA Medical Center, where I once served on the staff and faculty of the Head and Neck Division.

Examples from UCLA include the following:

- Gerald Berke, M.D. diagnosed several patients with SD who were cured after pursuing DVR with me. (Names of all patients are with consent.) He referred Gayle Pace who he had diagnosed with severe Adductor/Abductor SD. I referred her back to him within a month with a normal voice. Ms. Pace remains cured 14 years after treatment. The Reverend Henry Sellers was diagnosed with SD by Daniel Truong, M.D. and given a Botox shot that was ineffective. The Reverend Sellers tried UCLA Medical Center and Dr. Berke referred him to my private practice. The Reverend Sellers remains cured after more than five years despite the complications of Parkinson's disease. Dr. Berke diagnosed another patient with SD, Robin, who opted for DVR and has been cured for four years. Another patient he diagnosed with SD, Denise, was 95% better after a short time with my DVR program.
- Paul Ward, M.D., a former Chairman of the Head and Neck Division at UCLA Medical Center, diagnosed Marjorie Whitman with SD so severe that he recommended surgery. Ms. Whitman declined. She tried my DVR program. I referred her back to Dr. Ward with a normal voice. She remains cured of SD for years.
- Ed Kantor, M.D., who is also affiliated with the Cedars-Sinai ENT Division, diagnosed Lisa and Don with SD. Lisa was cured of SD after working with me 25 years ago, and Don has been cured for 15 years.
- Robert Feder, M.D. diagnosed Ms. Z with SD and advised surgery. She was referred to me and has been cured of SD for over 20 years.
- Hans Von Leden, M.D., now affiliated with USC, then UCLA, diagnosed SD and referred Dr. T. who has been cured for over 30 years. He also referred a second patient diagnosed with SD who has been cured for years.

- The late Henry J. Rubin, M.D., who was affiliated with Cedars-Sinai as well as UCLA, referred four patients he diagnosed with SD, all cured by DVR over a period of years.
- In perhaps the most telling referral from the UCLA's Head and Neck Division, one of its laryngologists referred his wife to me for treatment of her SD because he preferred my non-invasive treatment. She regained a normal voice through DVR.

With these 15 dramatic cures involving the UCLA Medical Center alone and since SD is ostensibly incurable, some have asked, "Did these patients really have SD?" I can only say that the renowned laryngologists at UCLA, "the Best in the West," diagnosed the SD patients that I treated in my private practice.

These examples can be multiplied by my cures of many other patients diagnosed with severe SD at other leading medical centers including USC, Cedars-Sinai, Scripps, Mayo Clinic, Vanderbilt Medical Center, University of Michigan, University of California San Francisco, and other facilities. I have helped post-Botox and post-surgery SD patients to achieve cures by DVR.

- Arnold Aronson, Ph.D. of the Mayo Clinic, for example, diagnosed The Reverend James Johnson with severe SD. The Reverend Johnson recovered a normal voice after he pursued a one-month program of DVR rather than undergoing the recommended surgery. He has remained cured for 20 years. Dr. Aronson confirms the cure.
- Ron was diagnosed with SD at the Mayo Clinic and treated elsewhere with five Botox shots, all ineffective. Ron is cured from SD by my DVR program.
- The Scripps ENT Clinic in La Jolla diagnosed Ginger, a young lady in her 20s with Spasmodic Dysphonia. She was told that her condition was hopeless and that she required lifelong series of Botox shots. My program of DVR gave Ginger a normal effective voice and she has remained cured of her SD.
- Dr. Hess, an emergency room medical doctor was diagnosed with severe SD by her laryngologist. He referred her to me. She underwent a program of intensive DVR and remains cured of SD for four years.

- Identical twins were diagnosed with SD at a well-known medical center, one with Abductor and Adductor SD and the other with Adductor SD. They were told SD was due to genes and was incurable. Both tried Botox. Both underwent my intensive DVR program and were successful in finding excellent voices.
- Kim was diagnosed with Adductor/Abductor SD by Dr. Norman Hogikyan at the University of Michigan. Botox shots were ineffective. She tried a month of intensive DVR and has been cured of SD for more than six years.

Dr. Rubin, whom I mentioned above, was a participant in two workshops at Cedars-Sinai Medical Hospital in 1982 and 1990 at which I presented patients with confirmed severe SD who told of recovering their voices through DVR. Dr. Rubin said, "We know you are the only one successful by speech therapy. Why?" I replied, "I do not do speech therapy; I do Direct Voice Rehabilitation." Dr. Rubin provided this testimonial:

> In the fifteen years immediately preceding my retirement from the active practice of otolaryngology, I have referred my patients in need of voice rehabilitation to Dr. Cooper because his results proved to be the most consistently satisfactory. His methods seemed essentially quite simple, in fact to the point of sometimes challenging believability, but they worked. He explains these methods in his book (*Modern Techniques of Vocal Rehabilitation*), and I believe that any voice therapist who gives them a serious and unbiased trial will be agreeably surprised.

Other authorized testimonials about my voice rehabilitation techniques include those from the late Lee Edward Travis, Ph.D., one of the founders and a past president of the American Speech-Hearing-Language Association ("He's the best in the business"); Robert H. Rand, M.D., professor of neurological surgery, UCLA Medical Center ("I found him to be really excellent"); and the late Joel J. Pressman, M.D., former chairman of the Head and Neck Division, UCLA Medical Center ("Dr. Cooper is the best speech pathologist I know").

Jack Pressman is my hero. It was his strong support and total commitment to success that allowed me to develop DVR. He told me, "Bring me success, not theories." I did. Without Jack Pressman, I would not have been able to find cures for spasmodic dysphonia, unilateral cord paralysis, and other voice problems through all-natural DVR, which I have reported in peer-reviewed publications. I owe my career to Jack Pressman, and the privilege of being part of his medical team.

I am grateful to my celebrity patients and others for their permission to release their names and to the ENT doctors who have availed themselves of my services to assist their SD patients by DVR. Henry Fonda, Shadoe Stevens and Keith Erikson all were diagnosed with SD and cured by my DVR program. Mr. Fonda went on to star in <u>On Golden Pond</u>, for which he won an Oscar.

I believe that any patient who has been diagnosed with spasmodic dysphonia, suspected SD or any other voice disorder should be told of Direct Voice Rehabilitation. DVR is a way to achieve a cure, recovery or improvement, especially since DVR is non-invasive, and dramatic results may be observed after a brief period of treatment. SD is curable by DVR. The SD patients have medical and hospital records indicating they have neurologically diagnosed SD.

I have been in full-time private practice for 35 years, and have presented lasting cures of severe SD at the Pacific Voice Conference in 1998, at California Speech-Language-Hearing Association Conferences, and at American Speech-Language- Hearing Association National Conferences in 1974, 1979, 1980, and 2000. In 1979, I received a Certificate of Appreciation "In recognition of a significant contribution to the American Speech- Language- Hearing Association and to the Profession of Speech Pathology and Audiology."

I have written books and chapters for professional handbooks and have published in medical/scientific journals on voice disorders. I also published an account of my cures and recoveries from SD in a peer-reviewed report in the *International Association of Logopedics and Phoniatrics* in 1980.

A chapter from my latest book, *Curing Hopeless Voices, The Strangled Voice (Spasmodic Dysphonia) & Other Voice Problems with Direct Voice Rehabilitation, An Alternative to Botox* (©2006), as well as chapters from my book *Stop Committing Voice Suicide* on SD and other troubled voices are on my web site, as are articles on SD and DVR as well as testimonials. For those interested in the cures and recoveries of SD by DVR, an audio and a video of my SD patients before and after DVR are available. I invite you to listen to the voices of cured SD patients before and after DVR on my website: www.voice-doctor.com. I also have a new DVD and VHS tape of cures of SD. This letter is intended to provide meaningful information for educated judgment regarding the treatment of spasmodic dysphonia and other troubled voices through Direct Voice Rehabilitation. I welcome your views and comments.

Cordially yours,
Morton Cooper, Ph.D.

P.S. I was invited back to the University of California October 18, 2008, reporting cures of Spasmodic Dysphonia with additional cures by Direct Voice Rehabilitation.

Notes About The Author

*Dr. Cooper's comments to himself.

August 26, 2005

I grew up on the streets of NY City, in the Bronx, in a poor section of the borough.

When my father died, I was eight years old. The Rabbi told me, when I asked, "why?"
"Because, God willed it."
"Could I talk with God?" I asked.

"No," he answered, "nobody talks with God."

My father was proud of being a Jew. My grandfather came from Odessa, Russia to escape the Czar and the Pogroms. I was ten when I asked him grandfather, "Why did you come to America," and he said, "because of the Pogroms."

I corrected him, saying, "You mean programs, grandfather?"
No, he answered, Pogroms.

I did not talk in class growing up. I had nothing to say. I found school excruciatingly boring. The class went as slow as the slowest in the class.

I went to DeWitt Clinton high school. I made myself invisible in class. I listened and said nothing. I saw what happened to those who spoke up. Three of my pals told our home class teacher, 'we want to take the college entrance exams" and she signed them up.
"Maudy is going too," they said.
"He is mentally retarded," she said without malice.
She signed me up because my pals said, "I had the legal right to take the exams."

They went but didn't take the exams. They just wanted the days off. I took the exams to Brooklyn College and City College. I passed both, and tried City College, left it because I had no idea of accounting, in the 23rd Street City College. I went to Brooklyn College. It gave me a liberal education, and the chance to engage my mind and find the world.

I volunteered for the service when I graduated from BC. I graduated second of a large number in the signal corps at Camp Gordon, GA. I was FBI cleared and went to the Pentagon. I was found to have ears to hear code beyond anyone's belief. I returned home having served in Europe at the American Forces Network.

I got a Teaching Assistantship (TA) grant from Indiana University.

I was interested in voice use because I was suffering a bad voice that made me see twelve MDs, and four speech therapists. I was thought to be strange. I complained about my voice. It hurt to talk, and my voice ached. I had seen ENTs in the service, and they were no help. I took a course in laryngeal anatomy and got an A. It didn't help my voice. I applied for a scholarship to Stanford, and within two weeks, was given one.

At Stanford, a high official in the admissions office met with me. He wanted to know why I got a scholarship to Stanford. I shrugged, telling him I wrote a five-page letter to Virgil Anderson, the Director of the speech Pathology Division.

"And?" he asked.

I told him how bad the voice field was citing my own case, and my journey thru the medical field and speech therapy field, and found no help for my bad voice.

"And?" he continued.

I told him the secretary who typed the letter said, "if Anderson answers you, he is crazy, and if you get a scholarship, you don't owe me a penny for typing your letter."

I showed her the scholarship letter but I didn't ask for my money back. She thought Anderson was nuts, and didn't think much of me, either.

The admission's officer asked me to "turn this way" and then "that way," gesturing so he could see me.
"You don't look Jewish," he said.
I concluded our meeting putting my hand out which he instinctively responded with his hand, grasped him to my face, and whispered in his ear, "I got admitted to Stanford, sir, because of brains." Looking back at him, he sat perplexed, and I laughed to myself. He hadn't dented me, and I had of him.

Anderson said I did the best job with stutterers in the history of Stanford University. He invited me to remain at Stanford but I had to wear a tweed jacket and tie. I wore neither. I turned his offer down, though he promised me a substantial increase in more money as in academia, a stipend.

I applied to UCLA and passed their entrance exam, and arrived there in 1961. Dr. Elsie Hahn ran the speech pathology division. She met with me for one minute.

"You want your Ph.D.?" she said. I nodded, yes.

"You work for Dr. Jack Pressman, the Chair of the ENT there at the medical center."

I demurred.

I wanted to get my Ph.D. as fast as possible.

"Your chances of getting a Ph.D. if you don't work for Dr. Pressman is zero to nothing."

I took the job.

"Dr. Pressman is waiting for you. You have five minutes to ask questions to get to the medical center and his office and you have ten minutes walk there." She smiled sweetly and gestured me out.

Outside the door a sober dark suited gentleman who told me his name motioned me to his office a few doors down the hallway.

"Sit down" he told me. I preferred to stand, and told him so.

"Sit down."

I sat.

"You want your Ph.D.?" he asked.
I nodded, yes.

"Here we wear a suit and a tie. Any questions?"
I nodded, no.

He motioned me out.

I had fourteen minutes and a half to get to Pressman. Charles Lomas the dark suited gentleman, thirty seconds.

I arrived at Pressman's office on time, but his secretary said, "You have to make an appointment well in advance to see Dr. Pressman."

I told her, "Dr. Hahn had sent me over," and was heading out the door when she shouted, "Dr. Pressman will see you."

He motioned me to sit down. I preferred to stand. He motioned me with his finger, sit down. I sat. "Bring me success, not theories," he said.

I nodded.

"You understand that?"

I nodded, yes, I understood.

I hadn't known he fired speech therapists who didn't bring him success. He wanted success badly. He was the school's most powerful doctor at UCLA Medical Center behind Mellankopf, the Dean.

He motioned me out. That took one minute.

Two and half minutes with three top people and I was on my way through UCLA for my Ph.D.

I finished my coursework in two years, but Hahn said, "You have to take another year else you will embarrass other Ph.D. candidates." I was about to walk. My wife pleaded with me, don't.

"Stay and get your Ph.D.," she said.

She had a MA from Stanford. I had told Anderson, she was brighter than I and when he met her, and reviewed her record, he agreed and gleefully told me having doubted my attempt to get her a scholarship.

Why do I tell you all this? Because I am a person who believes in ethics and morality and practices all that religiously. It is out of style today, but then, so am I and have been for years.

If you read the enclosed pages on what I have accomplished in the field of voice, perhaps you might have a clearer idea of who is bugging the hell out of you, your staff and the medical world.

I do not expect you to change your mind about cures of Spasmodic Dysphonia (SD), nor your position on Botox as giving those with spastic vocal cords back their voices. I am simply presenting what a no account kid with no background has accomplished against all odds, and who remains true to himself above all else and wishes to help people not snow them, and provide choice of treatment when medical care fails, and provide choice, as anyone would want.

I am sorry to disagree and fault your position on spasmodic vocal cords and on Spasmodic Dysphonia.

Though the medical field remains unable to cure SD ever, in over 135 years, and speech therapy, too, I am proud of reporting ongoing cures of SD year after year for 35 years documenting what I do, by Direct Voice Rehabilitation (DVR) all natural voice care.

Sorry to trouble you with this memoir, but I just won't let power, and the medical profession, and academics, and the drug folks run my life, my career, and me. When I read the *NY Times*, I expect the world. I am sorry you aren't providing it.

*Dr. Cooper's comments to himself.

September 5, 2005

Medical theories and drug causes have not reported a single cure of Spasmodic Dysphonia (SD) and Direct Voice Rehabilitation (DVR) all natural voice rehabilitation reports ongoing cures of SD for 35 years ongoing.

Dr. Morton Cooper, a solo practitioner has reported ongoing cures of SD and other hopeless voices cured by all-natural non-medical approach…

Dr. Cooper answers the medical and academic and drug related litany, SD is incurable, if it is cured, it wasn't SD, if it were SD, the cure won't last, and if the cure last, it couldn't have been SD because SD is incurable. Dr. Cooper has proven lasting cures of SD.

The humorous tales of what one doctor encounters in his treatment of SD and his cure of the hopeless voices that are Botoxed for life and surgically draconically treated and Russian Roulette outcomes while one doctor observes with whimsy, and humor what his today's colleagues in medicine, the pharmaceutical companies, and academia remain firmly planted in dark age treatment of SD and other hopeless voices.

The basis for today medical neurological model is a study done in 1960, Robe Brumlik and Moore which according to today's medicine showed that SD was a neurological problem. The study was inconclusive and it has limited cases. It became the rage in medicine without meaningful findings. There is no clinical evidence to verify SD is neurological, let alone a medical problem.

The Botox voice has replaced draconic surgery, which the *New York Times* in the Jane E. Brody column in 1992 purported to assure all that SD is incurable and surgery and Botox the treatment of choice assuring all that SD was not a misuse of the voice problem. *The New York Times* has continued to flog the belief that SD is incurable in the face of cures of SD by Dr. Morton Cooper.

Were it not for the drug company's money and power and reach, patients with SD would be given choice of treatment. But money influences, and PR does wonders to carry the day and tell all with SD, SD is beyond a cure, beyond understanding and presents ongoing failed medical theories and academic theories that never report a single cure of SD.

These theories includes: 1) neurological, 2) dystonia, 3) chemical brain imbalance, 4) dysfunctional basal ganglia, 5) gene related disorder, 6) psychiatric, 7) gastro esophageal reflux disease (GERD), 8) molecular biology.

Don't eat peaches, chew on a golf ball, shower and have hot water on your neck for strangled neck muscles, and strangled voices, and these outlandish beliefs are from the best and the brightest in medicine and were they known would be the laughing stock of what is medical voice SD care in the name of medicine.

Botox for SD is the rage today and has no cures ever.
It is Russian Roulette and its outcomes, four to ten times a year or more each and every year for life is as dark age as one dares get, all in the name of medicine.

And a fee of one, two, three, four thousand dollars a Botox voice shot helps fuel the disincentive to look elsewhere for an answer, a non-medical proven answer to SD and ongoing cures of SD by DVR. The medical drug academic juggernaut remains in place with SD told SD patients that SD is incurable, take your medicine, take your Botox, one of the world's deadliest poisons if not the deadliest poison, made into attenuated therapeutic doses that are uncertain in the Botox shot despite the well intentioned National Spasmodic Dysphonia Association (NSDA) given money by Allergan the maker of Botox to assure all that dosage is precise, when the Botox voice in dosage is experimental, and the Botox voice Russian Roulette, by the best and the brightest.

The *New York Times* is firmly behind the Botox voice and surgery despite the fact that 2/3 of those surgically treated by a fashionable procedure now believed to be in the dustbin of history with 2/3 of those surgically treated worse off than before the surgery, still ongoing surgeries with twists and turns for that procedure are ballyhooed by the best and brightest in medicine without a single cure ever.

God help our voices.

The best and the brightest and the best of drug companies will not allow cures of SD into its meetings these days. It isn't what today's medical SD voice care is interested in. Turf, ego, money, and more are basic components of why the medical care of SD remains incurable in the face of ongoing cures of SD by all natural DVR. One doctor against all medicine, the drug complex, and speech therapy (academia). One doctor versus all.

Merck's study in 1992 reported bad and raspy voices were related to acid reflux. Dr. Cooper's clinical practice does not find confirmation of the Merck Study in ongoing patients trying reflux drugs for bad and raspy voices.

SD patients and medical doctors do not report a cure of SD prescribing acid reflux drugs.

SD is medically now believed to be caused by acid reflux as one of the theories.

And Allergan's Botox, Bo for Botulism and Tox for Toxin, with the best of intentions, the most humanitarian of motives, and the most compassionate of purposes, acid reflux as a cause of SD among the varied theories that fail to cure, and were it acid reflux caused, as SD patients are prescribed acid reflux drugs from various drug companies in the name of medicine, SD would long have become cured. Not a single cure by acid reflux drugs.

Not a single medical cure of SD by Botox.

Not a single cure of SD dating back to 1871 when SD was first described by Traube as nervous hoarseness.

Nervous hoarseness?

If you hear the voice, you know why it was characterized as nervous hoarseness. It sounds like the patient is nervous, frightened, crying, or terrified. None of these characterized descriptions is true. It is the sound that makes people hearing SD people believe SD people are nervous and more.

Change the use of the voice, you change your life for the better and if you are disciplined and persistent, you have a chance, for a cure of SD by DVR, all natural voice help. Speech therapy has failed to cure SD because it doesn't treat SD in an orderly rational basis.

DVR takes the SD voice step by step out of SD, the deep throat voice that always is in the lower throat about the vocal cords and places it in the face, and does what nature asks, talk in the face, and it is the saving grace.

In 1991, I was on an Allergan sponsored meeting in Irvine, CA. My topic hadn't been presented, and when I did present my topic, I was off the panel of eight best and brightest medical specialists in ENT and neurology. My topic was cures of SD by DVR for twenty years. None of the panel ever reported a single cure of SD, and none have since then but then, none in medicine or the drug related field or academic report a single cure of SD, and insist SD is beyond a cure. It is beyond a cure for them and for the medical drug juggernaut, and my field, the academics, in the American Speech-Language and Hearing Association (ASHA). I report ongoing cures of SD for 35 years.

In peer publication, and at meetings before the Botox juggernaut took hold and before the powers in medicine and the drug field took hold and silenced cures of SD by all natural DVR.

In 2000, October 14, the NSDA sent a representative to me and she demanded I see her at once. She asked that I recant my peer review cures in 1980. The NSDA charter on its masthead says it is not to take treatment sides. It does.

The next month I was reporting cures of SD at ASHA, the national communication field. I had reported cures of SD dating back to 1974 in ASHA, and over the years in 1980, and in peer publication 1980, in the *International Association of Logopedics and Phoniatry.*

My presentations of cures of SD have been made at the California Speech-Language and Hearing Association (CSHA), at the top medical meetings, and the power of medical and drug funding has been able to disallow SD patients choice of treatment informed choice, and SD patients are assured by that there are no cures of SD. A guarantee by medicine and drug representatives that is not true. But as in ancient Greek times, in Plato's Republic, Thrasymachus answers Socrates about ethics that ethics should prevail, does not might make right?

And as then, and before, and throughout time, might does make right, and money talks and cures of SD are silenced for the best of intentions, the best of motives, the best of and brightest of minds in medicine and academia, leaving SD patients to endure and suffer SD with draconic Botox shots for life, with Russian Roulette the name of that game, and surgery no better all with the best of motives and intentions.

The psychiatric field has failed to cure a single case of SD. The neurological field has failed to cure a single case of SD.

DVR, the only approach in the world has proven there are cures of SD, reports them, and is disallowed to present them at today's medical meetings, and drug organized meetings on SD.

SD patients are not given a choice, an informed choice of SD care.

That is the problem with the medical and drug juggernaut and my field, ASHA, that has been taken over by drug company and proclaims to the world officially on its website, there are no cures of SD, and Botox the treatment of choice. It isn't so, but money talks, power rules, and the mighty prevail with failed medical theories and failure to cure as DVR all natural voice rehabilitation remains beyond the knowledge of SD patients, and off the radar screen of the media and the public.

God help our hopeless voices.

The blind lead the lost on SD and it remains incurable.

I remain, one doctor versus all, with cures of SD versus the entire medical establishment, the drug field and academia.

A metaphor for life, said a patient with a badly impaired voice, of being told, it was psychiatric, and this and that, and more when it wasn't all she was told, not this and that, and more but got her voice back by DVR and wrote of her experience.

Another patient found what he was told by the best and the brightest, and it was not of help until he underwent DVR, all natural, no-risk, and found his voice.

They are countless others with impaired and so-called hopeless voices have been cured of their voice problems, and live to tell about it.

*Dr. Cooper's comments to himself.

September 30, 2005

David Corcoran Science Editor, Assistant Editor of Science Times, "As I did with your previous letter, I'll pass the new one along to our health staff, I'm sure they will consider your comments when they revisit this issue."

Nick Wade, as former Editor of the *New York Times* Science Times wrote thirteen years ago, he would get back to me when they would revisit SD and its treatment and cause. That was regarding Jane E. Brody's one-sided ballyhooing of medical treatment for Spasmodic Dysphonia (SD), Botox and surgery and no cures of SD.

He didn't get back to me. The *New York Times* didn't either.

So I am publishing my exchanges with the *New York Times* and revisiting their silence about cures of SD by all natural Direct Voice Rehabilitation (DVR), and their endorsement, their full endorsement of "Botox giving those with spastic vocal cords back their voices."

The *New York Times* isn't interested in all natural DVR reporting ongoing cures of SD. "Botox is giving those with spastic vocal cords back their voices" implies a cure of SD. Botox for SD is not a miracle drug. "Botox is giving those with spastic vocal cords back their voices," is undocumented. Bo for Botulism and Tox for toxin, Botox is made to be the best money can buy. The newspaper, USA Today reported Tuesday April 20, 2004 was given information from the National Spasmodic Dysphonia Association (NSDA) that gets money from Allergan for its website, its newsletter and research reporting Botox for SD is the Cat's meow and a Godsend.

The next generation of injectables into our vocal cords from James Thomas, ENT,…and others. Collagen and interferon and silicone, and Teflon and bone, gel, and fat, and stents into the vocal cords as with Paraffin in 1913, are now passing fads and fashions that may be consigned to the dustbin of history, too?

Injectables are simply inserts into the vocal cords, seeking to provide structural fills seeking to give a normal vocal cord structure. Functionally is at loose ends.

Robert Kennedy Jr. has Botox as an injectable for his SD condition. Listen to his Botox voice does it give assurance in fulfilling what it promises, 99% effective and is it safe, too?

Meanwhile, an all natural voicelift, raising or lowering the pitch on ahem, without any invasive medical procedures or injectables does remarkably well but doesn't cost anything to speak of, and gives the voice back its normal natural voice simply and directly with a few other simple ways.

Is the ENT throat doctor and neurologist acting in the best interest of the SD patient? Have the ENT and Neurologists read of Dr. Berke's 1999, Dec. National Spasmodic Dysphonia Association statement: **In the December, 1999 National Spasmodic Dysphonia Association Newsletter, page 7, Dr. Gerald Berke, Chairman of UCLA Head and Neck Division reports regarding Botox (botulinum toxin): "...there are some obvious drawbacks. It requires lifelong visits from 4 to 10 times per year for repeat injections. The injections are not inexpensive. The interval between post injection breathiness, good voice, and the return of symptoms may not be very long in some patients. Hypersensitivity and antibody formation have been shown to produce some long term structural changes in muscle cells."

*Dr. Cooper's comments to himself.

October 4, 2005

Brin somewhere back in time asked me to write about psychiatric Spasmodic Dysphonia (SD). I declined. I wanted to write about so called "neurological" SD, because I don't find it neurological, but functional. Brin declined.

Meanwhile, the cover-up of cures at the *New York Times*, the best and mightiest of men…whose reporters take handouts from Brin, who sits on the Allergan payroll now as Senior Vice-President of Development was on the front page of the *New York Times* saying March 2, 2003 that Botox is the next penicillin.

Perhaps.

Allergan's CEO says in the *Los Angeles Times*, he wants Botox to perhaps be used for 93 different conditions… Dr. Brin ballyhoos Botox for SD, to treat the neurological cause. But SD I find reporting ongoing cures of SD is not neurological. Maybe the CEO would settle for 92 conditions that Botox best serves? Botox is one of the choices for SD, not THE treatment of choice, and the state of the art treatment in medical SD?

Thrasymachus and Socrates in the Republic clash over does, Might make Right and the issue is not resolved. Might does make Right, and always has.

Does the mighty *New York Times* care to use its might to right an oversight no cures of SD medically? My all-natural Direct Voice Rehabilitation (DVR), one doctor against all, takes on the entire medical establishment worldwide, drug companies, Allergan and Merck, and all academia, and friends, the National Spasmodic Dysphonia Association (NSDA). The NSDA is a sound alike Allergan, non-profit group that gets funds from Allergan to do chat rooms, newsletters, research, SD meetings. The NSDA decline to allow cures of SD by DVR, all natural, to appear at its national and international meetings.

The Botox SD shots have moved from one Botox shot in 1984 to four to ten or more a year, and the cost may be about 1,2,3,4 thousand dollars a Botox shot each and every year for life.

Isn't it time after almost fourteen years of correspondence with the *New York Times* to ask for an investigation of the *New York Times* hand me your Dr. Brin handouts, Brody, 1992, and March 2, 2003, and deny sourcing, who said "Botox is giving those with spastic vocal cords back their voices," front page Sunday *New York Times*.

It isn't the fallout of Botox for SD that is at issue alone. It is cures of SD that is.

Why does the mighty *New York Times* fault others for not balanced reporting? Yet they remain in self-denial of cures of SD when the documentation is provided them and the proof at their review, and not investigate? Not ever. The *New York Times* takes handouts from Allergan through Dr. Brin, now. Dr. Brin is a fervent believer in the neurological cause of SD. My clinical experience isn't in agreement. SD cannot be neurological. I cannot help cure a neurological problem. In 1845 Semmelweiss an MD found that the high death rate, more than twenty percent for child birthing was due to medical doctors not washing their hands. He was demonized. He lost his career, and standing in medicine. He is honored all too many years later as a great man. But how many women and children died before medicine came to realize, "wash your hands" during delivery of babies, was the right thing to do saving lives but not before?

The *New York Times* has been misled in the past. It has no mea culpa when it comes to cures of SD. It remains blind to cures of SD because it trusts in the medical model, the medial paradigm and the medical theories for SD that have not one single cure of SD ever covering 135 years dating back to Traube who characterized SD as nervous hoarseness.

SD is called the strangled voice. You know why those talking with such a frightening voices sound nervous. They are nervous. Not from being nervous but talking strangled and judged nervous talking so.

The neurologists and ENTs are not trained in practical voice use. They do not put the variables that make up a good and great voice to change from bad and strangled voices to a normal natural voice.

God help our voices. The medical profession hasn't, isn't, and if those in power and the mighty will not look into the matter, who will? Medicine has not, will not, and cannot police itself I find to openly discuss cures of SD, as neither will the Mighty *New York Times* do so…

It is the cover-up of cures of SD not only at the *New York Times*, but in the medical profession, and it is a David versus Goliaths story that cures of SD exist by all natural DVR and prevail as well, and that SD is mistakenly believed neurological when it isn't save a case here and there, as with psychiatric cause. DVR proves conclusively SD is subject to all natural cures, which may interfere with the bottom line of those in the cadre giving the Botox voice shots, and the drug companies involved in looking to medical cause. Who comes first? The SD patient or the drug companies and the medical people who do the Botox shots, and benefit from all of that?

And of the SD patients living a life of agony disabled of voice in a society where communication is key to fulfillment, left undone and on a roller coaster ride in and out, up and down, and around, endlessly for life?

Isn't informed choice something that we all seek for treatment? And cure?

*Dr. Cooper's comments to himself.

October 13, 2005

The Botox Voice and your car

If you fill your gas tank, you don't expect to find the gas carries you uncertainly for a few miles or doesn't carry you at all when you tank up and the engine fails so you are stranded each and every time you tank up.

Would you go back and get tanked up?

The engine fails each and every time you tank up.

Would you go back?

If you are told the gas is 99% effective but your car doesn't go, would you believe what you are told?

Yet, medicine with the best of intentions, with all the best of humane concerns, and compassion, tells you to get the Botox voice shot for your strangled voice and each time your voice goes out for variable periods of time leaving your voice less or so badly impaired you can barely be heard, or understood, as the state of the art and treatment of choice for your SD voice.

Does that make sense?

The Botox voice like pouring gas into your tank, leaves you stranded without a voice to get heard, listened to and liked. Something doesn't make sense. 99% effective when your car doesn't run smoothly after tanking up? Same for SD.

Your voice goes out, and the National Spasmodic Dysphonia Association (NSDA) tells you and me, the Botox voice shot is 99% effective when your voice regularly and consistently goes out each time you get a Botox voice shot. The NSDA gets donations of money from Allergan the maker of Botox.

You get the Botox voice shot four to ten times or more each year. And each time you get the Botox voice, your voice regularly goes out for variable periods of time. Would you back to that gas station over and over and over for life?

Botox voices are for life, each and every year for life leaving you without much of a voice after each Botox shot, but it is said to be the state of the art by medicine, and the treatment of choice by medicine. They in medicine know only medical voice care.

The *New York Times* entirely backs the Botox voice and reports on its front page March 2, 2003: Botox is giving those with spastic vocal cords back their voices.

Like those tanking up for their car, after doing so, the engine goes out each and every time, and that is called the best gas money can buy?

Something isn't right.

MORTON COOPER, PH.D.
A Speech Pathology Corporation

VOICE REHABILITATION
SPEECH AND LANGUAGE THERAPY

Westwood Medical Plaza
10921 Wilshire Blvd. #401
LOS ANGELES, CALIFORNIA 90024
(310) 208-6047 208-6748
FAX (310) 208-8737

March 16, 1992

Letters to the Editor
The New York Times
229 W. 43rd Street
New York, NY 10036

Dear Sir:

Jane E. Brody says in her (March 11, Personal Health) column on a voice disorder called Spasmodic Dysphonia, that the only effective treatment is surgery or Botulinum. Not so.

I have been reporting successes by my Direct Voice Therapy approach for the past twenty years at peer review meetings, in my textbooks and publications, and in my current paperback books, <u>Change Your Voice, Change Your Life</u> and <u>Winning With Your Voice</u>.

Of late, UCLA Medical Center has referred Spasmodic Dysphonic patients to my office, allowing me to continue to prove that Spasmodic Dysphonia may be effectively treated by my Direct Voice Therapy. The view that this voice disorder is always incurable is a myth. I have been able to show that Spasmodic Dysphonia is curable in cases diagnosed by the Mayo Clinic, by Stanford University, and by other medical referrals.

Edward A. Kantor, M.D., Chairman, Division of Otolaryngology, Head and Neck Surgery, Cedars-Sinai Medical Center, Los Angeles, has this to say: "Dr. Morton Cooper has shown unusual expertise in treating patients with Spastic Dysphonia. His methods of voice therapy in our patients afflicted with the markedly disabling disease have been highly successful."

I have presented recovered patients at Cedars-Sinai in 1982, and again in 1990.

Please, Ms. Brody, include Direct Voice Therapy as a possible option and alternative to surgery and Botulinum as a method of treatment of Spasmodic Dysphonia.

Most cordially,

Morton Cooper, Ph.D.

MC/ht

cc Jane E. Brody

MORTON COOPER, PH.D.
A Speech Pathology Corporation

VOICE REHABILITATION
SPEECH AND LANGUAGE THERAPY

Westwood Medical Plaza
10921 Wilshire Blvd. #401
LOS ANGELES, CALIFORNIA 90024
(310) 208-6047 208-6748
FAX (310) 208-8737

June 30, 1992

The New York Times
229 West 43rd Street
New York, NY 10036

ATTN: <u>THE PUBLISHER</u>

Dir Sir:

Jane E. Brody ran an article on the beauties of Botox (poison) for
the treatment of spasmodic dysphona. She neglected to mention that
voice rehabilitation may also be used in the treatment of this condition
despite the fact that she did have that information.

At a recent meeting of the National Association of Spasmodic
Dysphonics in Michigan, I understand from one of the sources there,
Jane Brody sent a nasty letter to Midge Kovacs who is a source for her
article.

I wrote a response to explain direct voice rehabilitation to your Letters
to The Editor Column- it never ran. I notice just in today's New York
Times, you have plenty of room to indicate that the new York Times is
a "blast," etc., but no time and no space for the many people suffering

from spasmodic dysphonia and who might benefit from knowing about a non-invasive, non-risk approach to their problem.

Enclosed is an article I did for a national journal association with the American Speech Hearing Association.

Don't you believe it behooves you to address a wrong committed by Jane Brody in the New York Times regarding my treatment of spasmodic dysphonia by direct voice rehabilitation?

I notice you have time for Resort Wear at the Seashore, Your Sister Wears Combat Boots, etc. I am a subscriber to the New York Times and read you daily. I love Your Sister Wears Coat Boots, too, but what about a little truth regarding approaches to spasmodic dysphonia other than invasive surgeries or poison injections.

Your Jane Brody article has made the round of newspapers across the country. The poisoning of America is in vogue with pesticides, herbicides, etc., and you decline to give voice to an approach other than poison and or surgery.

s there something I'm missing, sir?

Most cordially,

Morton Cooper, Ph.D,

MC/anb
Enc.

MORTON COOPER, PH.D.
A Speech Pathology Corporation

VOICE REHABILITATION
SPEECH AND LANGUAGE THERAPY

Westwood Medical Plaza
10921 Wilshire Blvd. #401
LOS ANGELES, CALIFORNIA 90024
(310) 208-6047 208-6748
FAX (310) 208-8737

July 3, 1992

The New York Times
229 West 43rd Street
New York, NY 10036

ATTN: <u>ARTHUR O. SULZBERGER, JR.</u>

Dear Mr. Sulzberger:

In today's New York Times, I found a few reminders by your paper
asking me to keep The New York Times in mind. You have space to
ask your readers to join with you so they get a real view of the world,
yet Jane E. Brody declines to give the readers of The New York Times a
perspective on treatment for spasmodic dysphonia.

One of the sources for the enclosed article written by Jane E. Brody
was Midge Kovacs, editor of OUR VOICE Newletter. I am enclosing
for your review and consideration the exchange that Ms. Kovacs had
with a support group leader in San Francisco who finds that driect voice
rehabilitation is relevant and that it can work for those suffering from
spasmodic dysphonia (enclosed item #1)

Item #2 is a letter I received from Muriel Paule today, July 3, 1992, which I ask you to be kind enough to review. Item #3 is Muriel Paule's permission to use the enclosed material.

At the 1991 Irvine meeting concerning spasmodic dysphonia, Dr. Mitchell Brin, the second source for Jane Brody's article dealing with poison for spasmodic dysphonia, said, I believe, and I am paraphrasing, that he would like to see Botox replaced at the earliest possible time in favor of another substance. That discussion and statement has not at any time, to my knowledge, been reviewed by Midge Kovacs' newsletter nor has it been discussed at other meetings concerning spasmodic dysphonia such as The Pacific Voice Conference in 1991.

You have two sources given to you that appear to be quite partial in what they are saying in the treatment of spasmodic dysphonia.

I am enclosing a video which depicts individuals who have recovered from spasmodic dysphonia by direct voice rehabilitation. It is said there are no recoveries -NONE- by my approach. This is inaccurate and misrepresents my experience and my published article from The International Association of Logopedics and Phoniatrics (see enclosed item #4.)

The New York Times has on its masthead, I believe, "All The News That's Fit to Print." I believe you are doing a disservice to the people who suffer from spasmodic dysphonia and are not given options to Botox and surgery. Botox has not been approved by the FDA for spasmodic dysphonia. Nobody knows the long-term down-side effects of this substance the body. My approach is non-risk, conservative and in keeping with the medical dictum: Do No Harm.

Would you be kind enough to investigate my position and if you find it valid, report it as such in one of your columns? Jane E. Brody declines to do so.

Nick Williams, past editor of the Los Angeles Times, was reported in your Obituary Column on July 3, 1992, as having said, "We have to be above even the shadow of suspicion that was ideologues."

I look forward to hearing from you.

Most cordially,

Morton Cooper, Ph.D.

MC/anb
Enc.

The New York Times
229 WEST 43 STREET
NEW YORK, N.Y. 10036

9 July 1992

Morton Cooper, Ph.D.
Westwood Medical Plaza
10921 Wilshire Blvd. #401
Los Angeles, CA 90024

Dear Dr. Cooper:

Thank you for your letter to Arthur Sulzberger, to which he has asked me to reply.

I read your paper on spastic dysphonia with great interest. As I am sure you understand, it is hard for our medical articles to be comprehensive reviews of the literature and we cannot mention every possible treatment. But I will pass your article on to my colleague Jane Brody for when next we return to the issue.

Yours sincerely,

Nicholas Wade
Science Editor

NW:ak

MORTON COOPER, PH.D.
A Speech Pathology Corporation

VOICE REHABILITATION
SPEECH AND LANGUAGE THERAPY

Westwood Medical Plaza
10921 Wilshire Blvd. #401
LOS ANGELES, CALIFORNIA 90024
(310) 208-6047 208-6748
FAX (310) 208-8737

July 15, 1992

Mr. Arthur Sulzberger, Publisher
The New York Times
229 West 43rd Street
New York, New York 10036

Dear Mr. Sulzberger:

Thank you for Nicholas Wade's letter of July 9, 1992 in response to my inquiry about mentioning my successes in treating spasmodic dysphonia by direct voice rehabilitation.

It seems to me that this is a round robin approach. I have already forwarded all relevant information to Jane E. Brody concerning my successes with spasmodic dysphonia by direct voice rehabilitation. I appreciate you sending it back to her, but for some unknown reason she declines to acknowledge my successes or existence dealing with spasmodic dysphonia by a non-invasive approach other than surgery or poison.

If there is any question you have concerning my background, my qualifications, my successes in dealing with this condition, please call or send an investigative reporter.

The New York Times cannot afford to be one-sided and mean-spirited toward approaches to any problem, let alone spasmodic dysphonia. The longer this one-sided approach continues, sir, the more people lack options and alternatives, as is with spasmodic dysphonia.

The New York Times has great integrity and it behooves you to correct the disinformation presented by Jane E. Brody in her article of March 11, 1992.

Thank you for your concern and interest.

I am enclosing additional material you may find of interest. Would you please be so kind as to return the textbook at your convenience as I am in the process of revising it.

Most cordially,

Morton Cooper, Ph.D.

MC/anb
Enc.

The New York Times

229 WEST 43 STREET
NEW YORK, N.Y. 10036

ARTHUR O. SULZBERGER, JR.
Publisher

July 22, 1992

Mr. Morton Cooper, Ph.D.
Westwood Medical Plaza
10921 Wilshire Blvd. #401
Los Angeles, CA 90024

Dear Mr. Cooper,

Enclosed is your textbook and video tape which you sent me. Let me assure you that I am in no way questioning your background or qualifications when I leave it to Times' reporters and editors to make decisions on such complicated matters as this.

In the end it is their call, and while I am pleased to bring information to their attention, I hope you understand when I say that I will not dictate to them as to what they should write.

Sincerely,

MORTON COOPER, PH.D.
A Speech Pathology Corporation

VOICE REHABILITATION
SPEECH AND LANGUAGE THERAPY

Westwood Medical Plaza
10921 Wilshire Blvd. #401
LOS ANGELES, CALIFORNIA 90024
(310) 208-6047 208-6748
FAX (310) 208-8737

July 27, 1992

Arthur O. Sulzberger, Jr., Publisher

The New York Times
229 West 43rd Street
New York, NY 10036

RE: <u>JANE E. BRODY:</u> <u>"POISON FOR A TROUBLED VOICE"</u>

Dear Mr. Sulzberger:

I am not asking anyone to dictate to any writer what should or shouldn't be said in any story; I am simply asking for objectivity and fair play. If that cannot be done in one column, it certainly can be done in another column or section of the paper which prints all the news that's fit to print, which is what The New York Times is all about, sir.

Thank you very much for your concern and interest.

Most cordially,

Morton Cooper, Ph.D.

MC/anb

PS Again, I asked for an investigative reporter to check out the fact that voice therapy does work for spasmodic dysphonia despite the fact that it is denied by the medical profession.

MORTON COOPER, PH.D.
A Speech Pathology Corporation

VOICE REHABILITATION
SPEECH AND LANGUAGE THERAPY

Westwood Medical Plaza
10921 Wilshire Blvd. #401
LOS ANGELES, CALIFORNIA 90024
(310) 208-6047 208-6748
FAX (310) 208-8737

September 22, 1992

The New York Times
229 West 43rd Street
New York, NY 10036

ATTN: <u>ARTHUR O. SULZBERGER, JR.</u>

Dear Mr. Sulzberger:

It was kind of your science editor, Nicholas Wade, to respond to my inquiry concerning an updated article on approaches to spasmodic dysphonia. His view is that "we are not going to write about it now."

Diane Bless, Ph.D., a professor at the University of Wisconsin, Madison, at the 1991 Pacific Voice Conference, told the audience that voice therapy was not effective for papillomata of the vocal folds. As I had done a study at UCLA Medical Center, which was published in a top journal in my field (see enclosed), I tried to correct the misconception that this presenter had. The chairperson of her presentation, Joel Ross, M.D., was of the view that the study was not biopsied. The study was biopsied. The two speakers left the audience with misinformation and disinformation concerning the effectiveness of voice therapy on papillomata of the vocal folds.

I have sent copies of the enclosed articles to both people; neither has seen fit to respond to my concern that voice therapy can be effective for this pre-malignant growth of the vocal folds.

Why don't these presenters correct this misinformation and disinformation now?

The American Speech & Hearing Association through its journal ASHA has written through an ethic committee (Jan Ciuccio) in August 1990 that testimonials are acceptable as ads, yet ASHA declines to run the testimonials of those who have recovered from spasmodic dysphonia by Direct Voice Rehabilitation.

Why not correct this misinformation and disinformation concerning the treatment of spasmodic dysphonia now?

ASHA did allow two Letters to the Editor, one, which I understand, is libel for a look-see by an attorney, attacking me for daring to present an open letter through ASHA's pages before they censored such means of me reaching out to speech pathologists to tell them that Direct Voice Rehabilitation has been effective curing spasmodic dysphonia. ASHA did not allow me to respond to the two negative letters at the time they were published, affording me a response some months later in its Letters to the Editor column.

Why not now?

Ms. Jane E. Brody, a gifted writer, in my view, has been flacked out by the medical view of those disorders and the treatment of those disorders.

I am writing to ask that you consider the possibility of utilizing a different perspective and different set of options and alternatives, not only for spasmodic dysphonia, but for all voice disorders. I differ remarkably with the treatment that should be afforded voice patients, as a voice pathologist contrasting to what is done by the medical community. The medical community has essentially no training in voice, let alone voice disorders. Ear-Nose-Throat doctors have but six hours in voice in their residency programs as Ear-Nose-Throat specialists. Yet, Ms. Brody is presenting the Ear-Nose-Throat doctors, such as Robert Feder, M.D. and others, as the mavens in the treatment of voice and voice disorders.

I would love to see Ms. Brody present a wider scope in her column on health in the treatment of voice and voice disorders and ask that she consider my input if and when she is so inclined to do such an article on the condition of spasmodic dysphonia for the pages of The New York Times.

Why not now?

Is The New York Times willing to abide with disinformation and misinformation when it is brought to their attention? Is this The New York Times I have honored and cherished all my life?

On the front page of the September 21, 1992 edition of The New York Times is the headline: FALSIFYING CORPORATE DATA BECOMES FRAUD OF THE 90'S. Historian, Richard Reeves, writes that lying is the current coin of our communication.

You indicate in blurbs throughout your paper: "...you sense your world is changing. Keep it in full view every day." What shall we keep in full view, sir, misinformation and disinformation?

Why not undo what is misleading and inaccurate, now?

You indicate in another blurb: "It's even better daily." What, may I pray, is even better daily — misinformation and disinformation?

I meant this to be a short answer to your response that "we are not going to write about it now."

If not now, when? And what of the people who don't know of options and alternatives to surgery and poison for spasmodic dysphonia or to voice problems in general, and don't get informed consent? What of them, now?

I appreciate your interest and concern about my interest and concern. I have a deep concern about the ethics, honesty and decency of where our nation is heading to, and I, for one, am not very happy with what I find and see, so you will forgive me for speaking up and asking when — just when — when will you speak up?

For your file, the gentleman who gave you the dolling up of poison in The New York Times, one of the two sources for Jane Brody's article, has been kind enough to ask me this past week to join with him in a study on the effectiveness of Direct Voice Rehabilitation on spasmodic dysphonia (see enclosed). The medical profession has kept me out of the conferences on spasmodic dysphonia and voice disorders — what point in naming names, but I would love to if you would care to investigate — and now have the temerity to ask me to train them, to show them how to find success with spasmodic dysphonia by Direct Voice Rehabilitation.

I have sent the audio/video of recovered patients by Direct Voice Rehabilitation to numerous professionals across the county because I have no outlet and no means of touching these professionals other than be securing the list of names and spending lots of my time and money to do so.

An article on what I do and how I achieve success with a problem that is incurable by medics and speech pathologists from the top of ASHA on down, as well as my treatment of voice disorders by simple, different procedures than my colleagues use, I believe, would be of interest to your readers whether in the health column or elsewhere.

If not now, when? If not me, who?

Whatever happened to The New York Times and its sense of conscience — does it remain only for its editorial pages?

Most cordially,

Morton Cooper, Ph.D.

MC/anb

cc Jane E. Brody
   Nicholas Wade, Science Editor

MORTON COOPER, PH.D.
A Speech Pathology Corporation

VOICE REHABILITATION
SPEECH AND LANGUAGE THERAPY

Westwood Medical Plaza
10921 Wilshire Blvd. #401
LOS ANGELES, CALIFORNIA 90024
(310) 208-6047 208-6748
FAX (310) 208-8737

September 29, 1992

The New York Times
229 West 43rd Street
New York, NY 10036

ATTN: <u>ARTHUR O. SULZBERGER, JR.</u>

Dear Mr. Sulzberger:

One of the 2 sources given to Jane Brody for her article on Botox for spasmodic dysphonia, Dr. Mitchell Brin, may be found in this month's <u>Vogue Magazine</u> on page 254: "Now a revolutionary new process is smoothing the most furrowed brows..."

The downside effect of this poison on the body is unknown. The FDA has not approved it, but there is a vast audience out there, apparently, that would be interested in any substance that provides hope.

The only question I have, sir, are people with wrinkles or poor voices getting informed consent?

Are the medical people providing Botox for wrinkled faces medical geniuses or medical buccaneers? I'm only asking.

The medical term for Botulinum Toxin is not poison, but Botox, a Madison Avenue term if ever I've heard one. I wonder if the good people providing this substance would provide it for their families and friends, if not themselves. Will the new motto of the 90's be: Have You Been Botoxed? Fads and fashions are made of less, sir, and as Lord Byron said, "If I laugh, tis that I may not weep."

With all good wishes to you and yours.

Incidentally, in a leisurely review of <u>The New York Times</u>, I found a few items advising me of the value of your newspaper. Would you not have room for an article by me talking about voice and treatment of such, like one of those Specials to <u>The New York Times</u> articles? The world is changing, as the blurb says, but what are we keeping in full view? Your blurb also indicates your newspaper is a great work-out for your body of knowledge — it depends on which body you are talking about, and the knowledge provided. The last blurb is Edge Closer for The Full Picture.

If not now, when?

Most cordially,

Morton Cooper, Ph.D.

MC/anb
Enc.

cc Jane E. Brody
   Nicholas Wade, Science Editor

beauty

adoring crowd. Martin Margiela's models stalked down the runway in somber-toned recycled clothing and looks of utter disgust. Masks of supreme indifference are practically ubiquitous on Japanese runways: the gloomy expressions of Issey Miyake's models naturally complement his shadowy silhouettes and shark-fin sleeves. At Comme des Garçons, every ensemble is accessorized with a pursed-lip pout.

America's love affair with the frown began in the forties, when world-weary sirens like Garbo and Dietrich ruled the screen and songs like "I'll Never Smile Again" topped *Billboard* charts. F. Scott Fitzgerald described standard behavior at Hollywood parties in his short story *Crazy Sunday*: "...there was no ghost of a smile anywhere; directly in front the Great Lover of the screen glared at him with an eye as keen as the eye of a potato." The neophyte paparazzi, due to the nature of their enterprise, elicited myriad celebrity scowls—and ushered frowns into the limelight. A decade later, stars like James Dean and Marlon Brando built careers on angst-ridden bravado.

Now, a revolutionary new process is smoothing the most furrowed brows

Frowners invariably send mixed signals. There are frowns of concentration, disapproval, concern, and malcontent—not to mention the polite frowns of those struggling to suppress a laugh. Some famous frowners had practical reasons to remain closemouthed. Of a peevish Elizabeth I, one sharp-eyed French ambassador noted: "Her teeth are very yellow and unequal...and on the left side less than the right."

Modern psychologists cite evidence that the mere gesture of frowning heats up blood flowing to the brain, causing an increase in negative feelings. Of course, the frown has always had its goody-goody detractors. The ancient Greeks even invented an avenging goddess, Nemesis, to thwart the insolent. More alarming, it now seems mothers of little scowlers may be partially right about the odds of faces "freezing that way": the frown—which uses forty-three facial muscles to a smile's paltry fifteen—is now considered a wrinkle-causing workout.

Happily, a revolutionary new process now being researched by a team at New York's Columbia-Presbyterian Medical Center is smoothing even the most furrowed brows. "People who frown a lot will inevitably get lines on their foreheads and around their mouths," says Monte S. Keen, M.D., Columbia-Presbyterian's director of facial plastic and reconstructive surgery. "And since a full frown usually involves squinting, they'll get crow's-feet, too." Eight years ago Andrew Blitzer, M.D., the hospital's acting chairman of otolaryngology (head and neck surgery), and Mitchell Brin, M.D., an assistant professor of neurology, began testing the use of Botox—a purified toxin from the bacteria that causes botulism—to relieve facial muscle spasms in patients with neurological disorders. What they found: when injected directly into a muscle Botox not only relieved painful spasms, but in weakening facial muscles, erased wrinkles, too, usually in just one treatment.

"This is a whole new concept in removing wrinkles," Keen points out. "The old ways were filling in the wrinkle, either with collagen, silicone, or the body's own fat; stretching it out with a face-lift; or actually cutting it out and sewing it up—where in essence you're trading a wrinkle for a scar."

Currently, the injections work best on lines on the forehead, crow's-feet around the eyes, and frown lines above the nose. "Little wrinkles around the mouth aren't yet appropriate for injections because the muscle weakness could adversely affect expressions like puckering or smiling," says Blitzer. A Botox treatment will take effect in one to three days and lasts four to six months. While the drug is not expected to be approved as an antiaging treatment for at least two years—"We need to work out dosages and duration of effects," explains Blitzer—it could give frowners something to smile about. ●

VOGUE BEAUTY ▶ 2'

MORTON COOPER, PH.D.
A Speech Pathology Corporation

VOICE REHABILITATION
SPEECH AND LANGUAGE THERAPY

Westwood Medical Plaza
10921 Wilshire Blvd. #401
LOS ANGELES, CALIFORNIA 90024
(310) 208-6047 208-6748
FAX (310) 208-8737

August 3, 1992

The New York Times
229 West 43rd Street
New York, NY 10036

ATTN: <u>JANE E. BRODY</u>

Dear Ms. Brody:

Enclosed is a before and after audio and video of patients who have recovered from spastic and spasmodic dysphonia by direct voice rehabilitation.

In an article dated March 11, 1992, you indicated that voice therapy does not work for spasmodic dysphonia. I hope that in a future column on a problem such as spasmodic dysphonia, you will be kind enough to report successes by me for this so-called hopeless voice problem by direct voice rehabilitation.

Direct voice rehabilitation treats the cause of spasmodic dysphonia which is misuse of the speaking voice.

Most cordially,

Morton Cooper, Ph.D.

MC/anb
Enc.

MORTON COOPER, PH.D.

A Speech Pathology Corporation

VOICE REHABILITATION
SPEECH AND LANGUAGE THERAPY

Westwood Medical Plaza
10921 Wilshire Blvd. #401
LOS ANGELES, CALIFORNIA 90024
(310) 208-6047 208-6748
FAX (310) 208-8737

August 7, 1992

The New York Times
229 West 43rd Street
New York, NY 10036

ATTN: <u>SCIENCE EDITOR</u>

Dear Sir:

I have previous correspondence with you concerning a condition
called the strangled voice, medically termed spasmodic dysphonia. The
medics believe there are no cures or recoveries from this condition. I
am enclosing before and after audio/video tapes with patients who have
recovered from spasmodic dysphonia by direct voice rehabilitation.
I have been doing this for the past 20 years at peer review and have
published in a journal associated with ASHA (American Speech and
Hearing Association), The Proceedings of the 18th Congress of the
International Association of Logopedics and Phoniatrics. Enclosed is
that article, as well, for your review.

Would you be kind enough to allow your readers to know that direct
voice rehabilitation is a do no harm option and alternative to surgery
and Botulinum poison as advertised in the March 11, 1992 column by

Jane Brody as the only way to go?

I look forward to hearing from you.

Most cordially,

Morton Cooper, Ph.D.

MC/anb
Enc.

MORTON COOPER, PH.D.
A Speech Pathology Corporation

VOICE REHABILITATION
SPEECH AND LANGUAGE THERAPY

Westwood Medical Plaza
10921 Wilshire Blvd. #401
LOS ANGELES, CALIFORNIA 90024
(310) 208-6047 208-6748
FAX (310) 208-8737

August 10, 1992

The New York Times
229 West 43rd Street
New York, NY 10036

ATTN: <u>ARTHUR O. SULZBERGER, JR.</u>

Dear Mr. Sulzberger:

Medicine and speech pathologists say there is no recovery from
spasmodic dysphonia by direct voice rehabilitation...

One in an on-going series to visit with you.

"...experts say the problem is not vocal abuse or strain." Poppycock.

Most cordially,

Morton Cooper, Ph.D.

MC/anb
Enc.

MORTON COOPER, PH.D.
A Speech Pathology Corporation

VOICE REHABILITATION
SPEECH AND LANGUAGE THERAPY

Westwood Medical Plaza
10921 Wilshire Blvd. #401
LOS ANGELES, CALIFORNIA 90024
(310) 208-6047 208-6748
FAX (310) 208-8737

August 17, 1992

The New York Times
229 West 43rd Street
New York, NY 10036

ATTN: <u>ARTHUR O. SULZBERGER, JR.</u>

Dear Mr. Sulzberger:

Gayle Pace was referred to me by the UCLA Medical Center, Head &
Neck Division with the most severe of all voice disorders, abductor and
adductor spasmodic dysphonia. By direct voice rehabilitation, within
three sessions, she recovered her speaking voice. I referred her back to
the medical center for a phonatory work-up, and they confirmed that
her voice was normal. You have her before and after voice on tape sent
to you previously of recovered spasmodic dysphonia patients by direct
voice rehabilitation.

The medics and speech pathologists say there are no recoveries from
spastic and spasmodic dysphonia. It isn't so.

I look forward to a column in The New York Times amending the
Jane E. Brody column of March 11, 1992 that declines to mention let

alone recognize direct voice rehabilitation as an option and alternative to surgery and poison, Madison Avenued as Botox for spasmodic dysphonia.

If you have any doubts about the recoveries from spasmodic dysphonia by direct voice rehabilitation, why not send an investigative reporter from your science section?

As a subscriber and reader of The New York Times, I admire your objectivity, and ask that you carry it over to the treatment of spasmodic dysphonia.

Most cordially,

Morton Cooper, Ph.D.

MC/anb
Enc.

cc Jane E. Brody
   Nicholas Wade, Science Editor

MORTON COOPER, PH.D.
A Speech Pathology Corporation

VOICE REHABILITATION
SPEECH AND LANGUAGE THERAPY

Westwood Medical Plaza
10921 Wilshire Blvd. #401
LOS ANGELES, CALIFORNIA 90024
(310) 208-6047 208-6748
FAX (310) 208-8737

October 6, 1991

The New York Times
229 West 43rd Street
New York, NY 10036

ATTN: <u>ARTHUR O. SULZBERGER, JR.</u>

Dear Mr. Sulzberger:

In your October 6, 1992 <u>New York Times</u>, page A14, your advertising department has expressed my view exactly. I wonder if you would be kind enough to give me the privilege to do what others have done, to express their opinions and views, though differing with the status quo of medicine.

Medicine's treatment of, not only spasmodic dysphonia, but voices, to me, is an adventure in wonderland. The medical treatment does not treat the cause, but rather the symptoms of voice disorders, not only spasmodic dysphonia.

The other day, I was in Sacramento at a group for spasmodic dysphonic patients. The individuals that I assisted at this meeting had been Botoxed already and still cannot talk, they have terrible voices, still strangled. I helped then to understand how to use the voice efficiently telling them, and you, that their prognosis is excellent by Direct Voice Rehabilitation. Yet I cannot be invited to the major meetings on spasmodic dysphonia and am ignored by the major players in the field of spasmodic dysphonia treatment which favors surgery and Botulinum Toxin.

The patients who I met with in Sacramento told me they did not know of the possible downside effects of Botulinum Toxin injected into their bodies. They do not have, and were not given informed consent. Is this in keeping with medicine's Hippocratic Oath: Do No Harm?

I wonder if you would be kind enough to let me do a piece on the O-Ed Page about a subject that would interest all of us — the speaking voice and why it goes wrong and how to treat it without invasive procedures for spasmodic dysphonia and/or the tired voice.

I am enclosing a copy of an article that the <u>Wall Street Journal</u> allowed me to present to its readers.

My title for <u>The New York Times</u> would be: Why The Speaking Voice Fails and What To Do About Its. If my title is not your title, I would be delighted to have you re-title it, but please allow me the privilege of presenting my point of view your readers o the speaking voice and why it fails us all too often. I estimate that at least 25% of us are losing our voices, if not many more. This is a sizable audience to reach out to and I hope you will allow me to do so.

A possible additional title might be: Medicine's Adventures in Wonderland for The Troubled Voice.

I believe you owe it to your readers to give them a full view of how troubled voices can be dealt with without invasive medical procedures.

Most cordially,

Mort Cooper

Morton Cooper, Ph.D.

MC/anb
Enc.

cc Jane E. Brody
   Nicholas Wade, Science Editor

MORTON COOPER, PH.D.

A Speech Pathology Corporation

VOICE REHABILITATION
SPEECH AND LANGUAGE THERAPY

Westwood Medical Plaza
10921 Wilshire Blvd. #401
LOS ANGELES, CALIFORNIA 90024
(310) 208-6047 208-6748
FAX (310) 208-8737

October 13, 1992

The New York Times
229 West 43rd Street
New York, NY 10036

ATTN: <u>ARTHUR O. SULZBERGER, JR.</u>

Dear Mr. Sulzberger:

Bill Clinton talked hoarse throughout almost the entire presidential
debate on October 121, 1992. Bill Clinton is an example of the medical
model going awry. I understand his medical advice is to take medication
for reflux, an acid that come fro the stomach supposedly over the vocal
cords creating hoarseness. I find this position untenable and irrelevant
to the hoarse voice he has. He is also being given allergy shots. Allergy
does not create his hoarse voice. He is talking with the wrong voice
from the wrong portion of his throat, the lower throat, this is what
is creating the hoarseness. He is directed to drink lots of water by the
medical model; it is irrelevant to his hoarse voice, I find. He is told to
rest his voice and to use it sparingly — all irrelevant, I find. The hoarse
voice basically comes from the misuse of the speaking voice. (please
see enclosed articles.) Bill Clinton's hoarse voice is due to his lack of
awareness as to how to use his speaking voice correctly and not, in my

opinion, caused by reflux, allergy, dehydration factors, etc.

Bill Clinton's voice problem is just the tip of the iceberg concerning medical treatment vs. voice rehabilitation for hoarse voice, if not spasmodic dysphonia itself. Governor Clinton has a painfully hoarse voice and yet the cause of that hoarse voice is really not openly discussed or reviewed which really is a must.

In your October 13, 1992 <u>New York Times</u>, you say, "Edge closer, get the full story, the big picture every day." May I suggest you honor this commitment in regard to Bill Clinton's hoarse voice and the medical model which, in my view, is contributing to the ongoing hoarse voice we are being treated to.

Enclosed are articles which deal with the hoarse voice which will give you an awareness of what I am talking about.

Bill Clinton's hoarse voice is in and is inundating us. It deserves a fuller story than just saying, Bill Clinton's hoarse voice... Please afford me the privilege of joining with you for the kind of story <u>The New York Times</u> is known to produce, a story of depth and objectivity, and such a story is called for in the case of Bill Clinton's hoarse voice.

Most cordially,

Morton Cooper, Ph.D.

MC/anb
Enc.

cc Jane E. Brody
   Nicholas Wade, Science Editor

MORTON COOPER, PH.D.
A Speech Pathology Corporation

VOICE REHABILITATION
SPEECH AND LANGUAGE THERAPY

Westwood Medical Plaza
10921 Wilshire Blvd. #401
LOS ANGELES, CALIFORNIA 90024
(310) 208-6047 208-6748
FAX (310) 208-8737

October 19, 1992

The New York Times
229 West 43rd Street
New York, NY 10036

ATTN: <u>ARTHUR O. SULZBERGER, JR.</u>

Enclosed is a letter sent to Daniel Truong, M.D., who is one of the leaders I providing Botulinum Toxin to spasmodic dysphonics. In addition, I am enclosing a memo from Dr. Truong sent to all spasmodic dysphonia support group leaders, a memo which speaks for itself, in my view, of censorship.

I do not believe that Dr. Truong would be found guilty of following Voltaire's advice: "I may not agree with a word you say, but I defend to my death your right to say it."

Most cordially,

Morton Cooper, Ph.D.

MC/anb
Enc.

cc Jane E. Brody
   Nicholas Wade, Science Editor

MORTON COOPER, PH.D.
A Speech Pathology Corporation

VOICE REHABILITATION
SPEECH AND LANGUAGE THERAPY

Westwood Medical Plaza
10921 Wilshire Blvd. #401
LOS ANGELES, CALIFORNIA 90024
(310) 208-6047 208-6748
FAX (310) 208-8737

October 27, 1992

The New York Times
229 West 43rd Street
New York, NY 10036

ATTN: <u>ARTHUR O. SULZBERGER, JR.</u>

Dear Mr. Sulzberger:

Henry J. Rubin, M.D., one of the foremost Ear-Nose-Throat doctors
in Los Angeles, retired recently, some five or seven years ago, I can't
recall. I had the privilege of working with him for about 15 years. He
had wonderful comments about the successes by my approach of Direct
Voice Rehabilitation to voice problems.

Dr. Rubin knew of my successes, as well, with spasmodic dysphonia,
and asked at a Cedars-Sinai Medical Group Meetings of Ear-Nose-
Throat Doctors why I was the only one reporting cures. My answer
was that I do not do speech therapy, I do Direct Voice Rehabilitation.
Medicine, today, says there are no cures for spasmodic dysphonia by
Direct Voice Rehabilitation, speech pathologists say the same. Henry
Rubin, M.D. and other M.D.'s knew better, but Henry said to me, and
I want you to know these famous words:

"After you are safely dead, everyone will be a Cooperian, and there will be statues to you."

I asked, "Couldn't I just fake it and come back and get some of the credit for the cures?"

"No," he replied, "you have to be safely dead, 25 years."

It's much more fun and better being credited for one's accomplishments in one's lifetime rather than getting the credit and the statues long after one can value such items.

I volunteered for the army after college, dear sir. I was the only one on the line trying to get in; there were 100 on the other line trying to get out. The psychiatrist who interviewed me though I was nuts trying to get in, pointing to all those who wanted out, asking, what does that say about me?

There is the right way, the wrong way, and the army way. Medicine has altered that to: the right way, the wrong way, and the medical way.

When will be now to alert the people who read <u>The New York Times</u> that poison, or Botulinum Toxin, nicknamed Botox, is already failing, and been failing. I have the patients to prove it and ask that you open your pages to investigate a non-risk, noninvasive approach that presents cures for spasmodic dysphonia. Do I have to be "safely dead" to have this story followed and investigated? Where is the news media when it comes to finding out what is really going on in medicine? You do a great job in all other areas of investigative journalism; what has happened to the medical section?

As Bill Clinton says, we need the courage to change, and as you are endorsing Gov. Clinton, I hope you can take these cudgels and follow through on this story.

Most cordially,

Morton Cooper, Ph.D.

MC/anb

cc Jane E. Brody
   Nicholas Wade, Science Editor

MORTON COOPER, PH.D.
A Speech Pathology Corporation

VOICE REHABILITATION
SPEECH AND LANGUAGE THERAPY

Westwood Medical Plaza
10921 Wilshire Blvd. #401
LOS ANGELES, CALIFORNIA 90024
(310) 208-6047 208-6748
FAX (310) 208-8737

November 2, 1992

The New York Times
229 West 43rd Street
New York, NY 10036

ATTN: <u>ARTHUR O. SULZBERGER, JR.</u>

Dear Mr. Sulzberger

For what it's worth, I long predicted Bill Clinton would lose his voice before Election Day. He is being treated by the medical model: don't eat dairy products, chocolate, junk food, and all that poppycock. I managed to get my position published in a local newspaper here, The Daily Breeze (please see enclosed.)

More to the point, I am enclosing a letter I sent to an editor in my field concerning the poppycock that surrounds spasmodic dysphonia, let alone the voice of Bill Clinton.

In the October 29, 1992 issue of <u>The New York Times</u>, in the Op-Ed Section, William Safire, in an essay, suggests we strike a blow for public disclosure. He was talking about pollution in the government and its agencies. I wonder if <u>The New York Times</u> would not strike a blow for public disclosure of the options and alternatives to poison and a filing surgical mode for spasmodic dysphonia?

Mr. Clinton's diet has nothing to do with his failing voice, I my opinion; and the basal ganglia has nothing to do with spasmodic dysphonia. The problem lies in the misuse of the speaking voice.

As Edward R. Murrow used to say, Good Night, and Good Luck.

Most cordially,

Morton Cooper, Ph.D.

MC/anb
Enc

cc Jane E. Brody
    Nicholas Wade, Science Editor

MORTON COOPER, PH.D.
A Speech Pathology Corporation

VOICE REHABILITATION
SPEECH AND LANGUAGE THERAPY

Westwood Medical Plaza
10921 Wilshire Blvd. #401
LOS ANGELES, CALIFORNIA 90024
(310) 208-6047 208-6748
FAX (310) 208-8737

November 9, 1992

The New York Times
229 West 43rd Street
New York, NY 10036

ATTN: <u>ARTHUR O. SULZBERGER, JR.</u>

Dear Mr. Sulzberger

Enclosed is the blurb in <u>The New York Times</u> which makes my day. It says you run interesting and often controversial articles in the Op-Ed Section.

My view of President-Elect Bill Clinton's hoarse voice is that he has had this problem for the past 15 years, and it is not due to the campaign, per se. His current treatment is that of diet, voice rest, shots, and herbal tea, of late.

I would like to do an article of the Op-Ed Page on the treatment of voices, President-Elect Clinton's voice being just one example of a medical model treatment. The treatment of voices concerns most of the people in this country and the delivery of that service for troubled voices is not working with the medical model.

Isn't there room for a <u>different view</u> of voice on the Op-Ed Page of <u>The New York Times</u>?

Most cordially,

Morton Cooper, Ph.D.

MC/anb
Encl.

cc Jane E. Brody
   Nicholas Wade, Science Editor

MORTON COOPER, PH.D.
A Speech Pathology Corporation

VOICE REHABILITATION
SPEECH AND LANGUAGE THERAPY

Westwood Medical Plaza
10921 Wilshire Blvd. #401
LOS ANGELES, CALIFORNIA 90024
(310) 208-6047 208-6748
FAX (310) 208-8737

November 23, 1992

The New York Times
229 West 43rd Street
New York, NY 10036

ATTN: <u>ARTHUR O. SULZBERGER, JR.</u>

Dear Mr. Sulzberger

William Safire has done a wonderful job in unearthing the facts concerning government improprieties. I believe the enclosed material may give you some idea of a one-sided approach by those who are reviewing the treatment for troubled voices, such as, spasmodic dysphonia.

Of the persona involved, Dan Boone is a Ph.D., a former president, the American Speech and Hearing Association, and a professor. Herb Dedo is an M.D. and a founder of a surgical approach to spasmodic dysphonia.

My response to Lynn Gold, I believe, speaks for itself.

In today's edition of <u>The New York Times</u>, Jane Brody had an excellent article on diet providing an objective analyses of the problem of dieting. I look forward to Ms. Brody doing an objective article on the treatment of voice disorders.

Most cordially,

Morton Cooper, Ph.D.

MC/anb
Enc.

cc Jane E. Brody
   Nicholas Wade, Science Editor

MORTON COOPER, PH.D.
A Speech Pathology Corporation

VOICE REHABILITATION
SPEECH AND LANGUAGE THERAPY

Westwood Medical Plaza
10921 Wilshire Blvd. #401
LOS ANGELES, CALIFORNIA 90024
(310) 208-6047 208-6748
FAX (310) 208-8737

December 4, 1992

The New York Times
229 West 43rd Street
New York, NY 10036

ATTN: <u>ARTHUR O. SULZBERGER, JR.</u>

Dear Mr. Sulzberger

I love your ad.

Most cordially,

Morton Cooper, Ph.D.

MC/anb
Enc.

Ambitious.
Articulate.
Available.
1-800-631-2500

MORTON COOPER, PH.D.
A Speech Pathology Corporation

VOICE REHABILITATION
SPEECH AND LANGUAGE THERAPY

Westwood Medical Plaza
10921 Wilshire Blvd. #401
LOS ANGELES, CALIFORNIA 90024
(310) 208-6047 208-6748
FAX (310) 208-8737

January 15, 1993

Mr. William Safire
The New York Times
229 West 43rd Street
New York, NY 10036

Dear Mr. Safire:

Dr Suen's response that the vocal cords swell from allergy is of interest to me as I do not find this type of situation occurring in my practice as a voice and speech doctor. The efficiency of the vocal cords is not affected by allergy; the character of voice or the tone may be. Medical people believe that allergy affects the vocal cords and have so believed for years and years. I differ with this view and position. Because of this view that allergy affects the vocal cords, Ear-Nose-Throat doctors continue the treatment of voice cases such as Bill Clinton's assuming that allergy is affecting the cords and not realizing that the problem is one of voice misuse. Allergies are all too frequent for most of us, but we do not have hoarse voices because of these allergies, I find.

Of late, the medics are finding a condition called reflux as a cause of the hoarse voice. Again, I suggest you view reflux as simply a problem that some individuals have but it need not affect the speaking voice.

The belief by the medical people that reflux, allergies, sinusitis, etc. are contributory causes to the hoarse voice does not bear with my experience for the past 30 years as a voice and speech doctor. I have dealt with patients who have been referred to me by medical associates and specialists who have treated hoarse voices just as Bill Clinton is being treated for his voice. By a program of Direct Voice Rehabilitation, a change of focus, not pitch, per se, a clear efficient voice emerges and holds.

In a study of 128 patients discharged from my office, 98% remain good to excellent up to seven years after discharge from therapy (please see enclosed.) This despite the fact that they encountered allergies, reflux, sinusitis, etc.

In your article , you indicate that Bill Clinton is in no danger of throat cancer. Maybe not, but he has had continued hoarseness for over 15 years according to a CNN profile of him that I viewed (see enclosed, also my textbook, <u>Modern Techniques of Vocal Rehabilitation</u>.) The real problem is not one of cancer per se, or polyps, or nodes, but the ongoing hoarseness and medical treatment for it. To me, Bill Clinton's voice is the tip of the iceberg concerning the medical treatment for voice in this country. The medical people, including Ear-Nose-Throat specialists, essentially have 6 hours of training in the speaking voice and voices in general; I suggest you check this out. Dr. Gerald Berke, head of the UCLA Medical Center, who joined with me on a television program I do said, it is true that Ear-Nose-Throat people have 6 hours of training in the speaking voice. Dr. Joel Shulman, an Ear-Nose-Throat doctor hear in Century City had the same view when he was interviewed on my program. As a former clinical assistant professor at the UCLA Medical Center with responsibility for training interns and residents in the field of medicine as well as Ear-Nose-Throat, it was my experience that the Ear-Nose-Throat people had an extremely limited number of hours in learning about the speaking voice, though they are the ones the public looks to with their troubled voices.

Dr. Wilbur Gould, the treating Ear-Nose-Throat doctor for Bill Clinton, in my view, can recognize a wrong voice, but his approach is that of a medical response. Clinton, in my view, if you listen to his December 22, 1992 press conference nominating Warren Christopher to the post of Secretary of State, is heading toward the strangled voice — spasmodic dysphonia. This, of course, is not nodes, polyps, or cysts, but a much more serious condition which I find of concern.

You say the President's <u>occasional</u> voice problem is apparently no big deal. His hoarseness has not been occasional, Mr. Safire, it has been ongoing for 15 years and I suggest you get a hold of the CNN profile and check for yourself. Listening may not be believing, but it may be the start of your awareness that Bill Clinton has had a hoarse voice for a long period of time.

In essence, how do we treat a hoarse voice: medically, or by a competent voice rehabilitation? I submit to you that the medical model is not doing the job in helping Bill Clinton to overcome his hoarse voice and his voice therapy may not be touching the right cord. His problem is that of focus, not pitch. Having been known in the field for many years as a high pitch man — a derogatory statement and view of me for saying that pitch is relevant and important in overcoming a troubled voice, contrary to Dr. Brodnitz who said, don't pitch the voice, it's dangerous. I suggest you look to focus, not pitch (see enclosed.)

I would be delighted to meet with you, I will be in New York next week, or please do not hesitate to call me if you have any questions.

The answers that you are getting from the medical people are one-sided in their treatment of the troubled voice. Are you willing to hear a non-medical approach that does wonders for the hoarse and troubled voice?

Most cordially,

Morton Cooper, Ph.D.

MC/anb
Enc.

MORTON COOPER, PH.D.
A Speech Pathology Corporation

VOICE REHABILITATION
SPEECH AND LANGUAGE THERAPY

Westwood Medical Plaza
10921 Wilshire Blvd. #401
LOS ANGELES, CALIFORNIA 90024
(310) 208-6047 208-6748
FAX (310) 208-8737

February 8, 1993

The New York Times
229 West 43rd Street
New York, NY 10036

ATTN: <u>ARTHUR O. SULZBERGER, JR.</u>

Dear Mr. Sulzberger

I have enclosed a one half hour program titled, "Cures For Spastic and Spasmodic Dysphonia" for your review. No one else is reporting success; I continue to report successes — cures for spasmodic dysphonia for the past 20 years by Direct Voice Rehabilitation.

Won't you please consider interviewing me on this issue? I would be glad to come to New York and join with you, Ms. Brody, Mr. Wade and Dr. Altman, your medical reporter.

President Clinton continues to talk hoarse and does so because he is talking wrong. The medical model is not helping him: diet, reflux, allergy treatment, steroids, etc. I believe he is heading toward spasmodic dysphonia.

I look forward to your early response.

Most cordially,

Morton Cooper, Ph.D.

MC/anb
Enc.

MORTON COOPER, PH.D.
A Speech Pathology Corporation

VOICE REHABILITATION
SPEECH AND LANGUAGE THERAPY

Westwood Medical Plaza
10921 Wilshire Blvd. #401
LOS ANGELES, CALIFORNIA 90024
(310) 208-6047 208-6748
FAX (310) 208-8737

February 12, 1993

The New York Times
229 West 43rd Street
New York, NY 10036

ATTN: <u>ARTHUR O. SULZBERGER, JR.</u>

Dear Mr. Sulzberger

Please read the enclosed statement by Mrs. Betty Kay Jonkman.
Also enclosed is a letter of referral from the chairperson of the UC
Sacramento medical section referring her to me with spastic dysphonia.
The medical view is there is no recovery from spastic dysphonia by <u>their</u>
voice therapy — not mine.

In my office, is a gentleman who has had a surgical procedure,
paralyzing the vocal cord. He has spastic dysphonia. He has had 2
poison shots within a few weeks of each other. He still cannot talk. His
prognosis in my office is excellent, despite what they have done to him.

Enclosed is a journal article that just came out telling what I do in
contrast to what other speech pathologists and medics are doing.

In the midst of world chaos, disasters everywhere, and Doctor Panglos (from Voltaire's <u>Candide</u>) saying this is the best of all possible worlds, I ask you to do a follow-up story in <u>The New York Times</u> about another way to treat spastic dysphonia, a non-invasive direct approach employing my therapy, Direct Voice Rehabilitation. Won't you please give patients who are enduring medical madness an opportunity to have informed consent — options and alternatives to surgery and poison?

I am terribly sorry to burden you with my concerns. I cannot change the world; I can change spastic dysphonia to a clear efficient voice, and nobody else will or can. The medics will not allow me in to tell and talk about what I do and <u>The New York Times</u> is the forum of entree to the medical world, speech pathologists, and the public. You are the best newspaper in the business, I ask that you give me the opportunity to add to that reputation.

Most cordially,

Morton Cooper, Ph.D.

MC/anb
Enc.
cc Jane E. Brody
    Nicholas Wade, Science Editor

The New York Times
229 WEST 43 STREET
NEW YORK, N.Y. 10036

19 February 1993

Morton Cooper, Ph.D.
Westwood Medical Plaza
10921 Wilshire Blvd. #401
Los Angeles, CA 90024

Dear Dr. Cooper,

Thank you for your two letters to Mr. Sulzberger, to which he has asked me to respond.

I must make clear that The New York Times cannot be the primary forum for announcing your treatment to the medical world. We cannot evaluate novel drugs or medical treatments. That is the proper role of qualified experts and medical journals. Sometimes even experts are wrong but that is another matter.

I and my colleagues Jane Brody and Larry Altman are well aware of your work and they will not hesitate to seek your expert advice when needed. I thank you for all your letters but could you now please rest assured that they have served their purpose and there is no present need for more.

Yours sincerely,

Nicholas Wade
Science Editor

NW:ak

MORTON COOPER, PH.D.
A Speech Pathology Corporation

VOICE REHABILITATION
SPEECH AND LANGUAGE THERAPY

Westwood Medical Plaza
10921 Wilshire Blvd. #401
LOS ANGELES, CALIFORNIA 90024
(310) 208-6047 208-6748
FAX (310) 208-8737

February 24, 1993

The New York Times
229 West 43rd Street
New York, NY 10036

ATTN: <u>NICHOLAS WADE</u>, Science Editor

Dear Mr. Wade:

I do not ask <u>The New York Times</u> to be "primary forum" for my
treatment of spastic/spasmodic dysphonia. I ask that <u>The New York
Times</u> balance its coverage on spastic/spasmodic dysphonia and voices
with a non-medical approach that produces cures from this condition.
The medical world has not a single cure of spastic/spasmodic dysphonia;
that is not my position, it is theirs.

I do not ask you to evaluate novel drugs or medical treatments; I
ask you to afford a proven method of approach to spastic/spasmodic
dysphonia by Direct Voice Rehabilitation, that has had peer review, that
has been published in the top speech pathology journal (International
Association of Logopedics & Phoniatrics.) In Jane Brody's column,
unless my eyes and mind are wandering, she did evaluate surgery and
Botulinum Toxin as being the only avenues of approach to spastic/

spasmodic dysphonia. If what you are saying is "We cannot evaluate novel drugs or medical treatments," then why push poison for spastic/spasmodic as the rage in medical treatment for this condition?

The denigration of Direct Voice Rehabilitation for spastic/spasmodic dysphonia by the medical community, I believe, will leave a bad taste when the history of spastic/spasmodic dysphonia treatment is written.

The fact that the medical community declines to listen, let alone respond to Direct Voice Rehabilitation and its cures and recoveries from spastic/spasmodic says all too much about the mind and direction of the medical community. The experts in medicine are creating a cottage industry with procedures and Byzantine "help" for spastic/spasmodic dysphonia cases.

How can I rest assured when patients are given 2 invasive procedures, surgery or poison, and do not know of the option and alternative: Direct Voice Rehabilitation for this condition? (A case in point is Mrs. Betty Jonkman — please see enclosed.)

A gentleman by the name of Emile Zola, as you know, addressed the issue of Dreyfus and the scandal that came about because of Zola's J'accuse is a scandal I see that will eventuate in the treatment of spastic/spasmodic dysphonia. As John Paul Jones once said, "I have just begun to fight," or should it be said, "I have just begun to write."

With all good cheer, I will not be silent,

Most cordially,

Morton Cooper, Ph.D.

MC/anb
Enc.

cc Arthur O. Sulzberger, Jr
   Jane E. Brody

MORTON COOPER, PH.D.
A Speech Pathology Corporation

VOICE REHABILITATION
SPEECH AND LANGUAGE THERAPY

Westwood Medical Plaza
10921 Wilshire Blvd. #401
LOS ANGELES, CALIFORNIA 90024
(310) 208-6047 208-6748
FAX (310) 208-8737

April 14, 1993

The New York Times
229 West 43rd Street
New York, NY 10036

ATTN: <u>ARTHUR O. SULZBERGER, JR.</u>

Dear Mr. Sulzberger

I hope all has gone well with you since last I've written.

I am delighted to find out about the chefs. On Wednesday, April 14, the Living Arts Section presented a wonderful article on chefs, as was Jane Brody's article on protecting your eyes. You have a Wine Talk segment, and a 60 Minuet Gourmet section, and quite often you have fashions. In the Living Arts Section today, I noticed the ad featuring a Moveable Feast indicating the hunger for knowledge — it is said nothing beats The Times for insightful coverage... and you list a number of areas of expertise, one among these areas is health. Botulinum Toxin continues to be the rage among medics — I call it poison, sir, medics call it Botox. With your paper declining to present an alternative therapy to this substance for spasmodic dysphonia, surgery and Botox are the mainstays of <u>The New York Times</u>' position on treatment for SD, I gather.

You have pages devoted to fashion, chef articles, wine talk, gourmet talk — couldn't you have voice talk allowing your readership a perspective on how voices can be treated non-medically, successfully with proven studies, as I have presented year-after-year in different publications?

Just asking.

I hope all goes well with you, Jane Brody and Nicholas Wade,

I believe it was Rabelais somewhere in the 16th Century who was alleged to have said, "Ring down the curtain, the farce is over." I wonder if that statement can apply to today's medicine and its treatment of spasmodic dysphonia and voices in general such as that of President Clinton.

Most cordially,

Morton Cooper, Ph.D.

MC/anb
Enclosure

cc Jane E. Brody
   Nicholas Wade, Science Editor

MORTON COOPER, PH.D.

A Speech Pathology Corporation

VOICE REHABILITATION
SPEECH AND LANGUAGE THERAPY

Westwood Medical Plaza
10921 Wilshire Blvd. #401
LOS ANGELES, CALIFORNIA 90024
(310) 208-6047 208-6748
FAX (310) 208-8737

April 21, 1993

Nicholas Wade, Science Editor
The New York Times
229 West 43rd Street
New York, NY 10036

Dear Mr. Wade:

In a letter dated February 19, 1993, you indicate to me you "cannot
be the primary forum for announcing your treatment to the medical
world." I do not ask <u>The New York Times</u> to be the primary forum
for announcing my treatment to the medical world; I am concerned
with the public. I have already published my cures and findings in
the top medical and scientific journals. Additionally, you say you
cannot evaluate "novel drugs or medical treatments." My recoveries
and cures of Paralytic Dysphonia, Papillomata of the vocal folds,
hoarse voice, Spasmodic Dysphonia, need not be evaluated as novel
as they are proven and of long standing duration. You and Jane Brody
have presented poison or Botox and surgery as the key approach to
Spasmodic Dysphonia. You were the primary forum for this novel drug
approach and medical treatment. I am simply asking you to balance the
perspective provided your readers in the treatment of voice disorders.

President Bill Clinton remains hoarse. The whole country is hearing that hoarse voice. You have indicated that you would not hesitate to seek my expert advice when needed.

Let me tell you about the study I have done in regard to the hoarse voice...

I did a study on the hoarse voice at UCLA Medical Center under the aegis of the medical center to seek answers as to why the voice goes hoarse. The study covered 155 patients. It was found that 150 of these patients talked too low in pitch and in the lower throat. I raised that pitch of voice and changed the focus to the mask around the lips and nose using a clinical tool called the "um-hmm." This simple clinical tool allowed me to find the efficient voice immediately without use of a pitch pipe, a piano, or any computerized instrumentation. A follow-up of the patients was conducted some 7 years after they were discharged from therapy. The findings were that 98% of the 128 patients followed up remained excellent or good.

This study involved a spectrographic analysis, which is a typical approach to determining the pitch of voice.

President Clinton has a hoarse voice and is not getting better by medical treatment.

Would it be asking too much of you to do a story on a proven technique that overcomes hoarse voice by my approach of Direct Voice Rehabilitation? This study involves clinical trials and the procedures I believe you are asking for to substantiate a method of approach to the hoarse voice. The same method, incidentally, is used to overcome and cure Spasmodic Dysphonia.

Additionally, another study that was done under medical aegis is Papillomata of the Vocal Folds which shows that this condition responds to Direct Voice Rehabilitation. Success of Paralytic Dysphonia by Direct Voice Rehabilitation was also done at the medical center.

Why not give your readers an alternative non-medical approach,
Direct Voice Rehabilitant, to the troubled voice, such as, hoarse voice,
Spasmodic Dysphonia, etc.? My advice does not include drinking lots
of water, taking poison, or having surgery. My cures and recoveries are
extensive.

I look forward to your response regarding this inquiry.

Most cordially,

Morton Cooper, Ph.D.

MC/anb
Enclosures

cc Arthur O. Sulzberger, Jr
   Jane E. Brody

The New York Times

229 WEST 43 STREET
NEW YORK, N.Y. 10036

28 April 1993

Morton Cooper, Ph.D.
Westwood Medical Plaza
10921 Wilshire Blvd. #401
Los Angeles, CA 90024

Dear Dr. Cooper:

    Thanks for your letter and interesting remarks on Mr.
Clinton's cough. I'm passing your letter on to my colleague Dr.
Altman who follows this matter closely.

Yours sincerely,

Nicholas Wade
Science Editor

NW:ak

MORTON COOPER, PH.D.
A Speech Pathology Corporation

VOICE REHABILITATION
SPEECH AND LANGUAGE THERAPY

Westwood Medical Plaza
10921 Wilshire Blvd. #401
LOS ANGELES, CALIFORNIA 90024
(310) 208-6047 208-6748
FAX (310) 208-8737

June 25, 1993

The New York Times
229 West 43rd Street
New York, NY 10036

ATTN: <u>ARTHUR O. SULZBERGER, JR.</u>

Dear Mr. Sulzberger

I thought I would take a moment to chat with you as it has been a while since that opportunity has come to pass.

In the Obituary Column of your newspaper, June 25, 1993, page B-16, the report if the passing of Anthony Standen is headlined as one who deflated pomposity. He wrote a book titled, "Science is A Sacred Cow" (Dutton, 1950). The book has remained in print for 40 years; apparently, he is saying something. A quote from your write-up is as follows: "Mr. Standen's point was that scientists, and especially teachers of science, tended to have inflated egos, certain of their superior wisdom and virtue. In reality, he asserted, they are mostly dull and pompous and should be laughed at now and then. Unfortunately, in his view, the general public stood in awe of them even when they talked Latinized nonsense."

Please forgive me for adding medical people, especially Ear-Nose-Throat doctors, and speech pathologists, especially those leading The American Speech and Hearing Association, as heirs to the condition that Mr. Standen described of scientists.

As I mentioned before, I am taken with articles on dining, chefs, and fashions of clothes, but not a word about cures of the strangled voice, or a mention of Bill Clinton's hoarse voice and why it remains as it is.

I love the blurbs that your newspaper runs such as the ones I have closed that provide self-praise for <u>The New York Times</u>. It seems to me to be a bit over-stated. I believe it was some poet who said, "The boast of heraldry/The pomp of power/And all the beauty/All that life e're gave/awaits, alas, the inevitable hour/The path of glory/Leads but to the grave."

Anthony Standen well knew that view and I believe that is what makes me respect him as well as his contributions in his field as a chemist. Your article indicated that he was irreverent. I, too, am irreverent and hope to help society.

Mr. Wade has said in one fashion or another that he will get back to me about doing a story on spasmodic dysphonia, or possibly Bill Clinton's voice. Did he mean this century or next?

It is a pleasure to read <u>The New York Times</u>, but I must tell you that you do not present the full story or the big picture of things.

Is <u>The New York Times</u>, so thin-skinned, sir, that it cannot consider an alternative therapy that is successful, or even bother to investigate such an alternative therapy? Howard Kurtz of <u>The Washington Post</u> was recently on Brian Lamb's "Book Notes" saying the newspapers pint fingers at others, but not yourselves.

I hope this chat finds you in good fettle, in good health. As for me, I am going down to McDonald's to have a hamburger and fries, and what with the Coke and Pepsi scare, I think I'll jut have straight water.

As ever, most cordially,

Morton Cooper, Ph.D.

MC/anb
Enclosures

MORTON COOPER, PH.D.
A Speech Pathology Corporation

VOICE REHABILITATION
SPEECH AND LANGUAGE THERAPY

Westwood Medical Plaza
10921 Wilshire Blvd. #401
LOS ANGELES, CALIFORNIA 90024
(310) 208-6047 208-6748
FAX (310) 208-8737

July 6, 1993

The New York Times
229 West 43rd Street
New York, NY 10036

ATTN: <u>ARTHUR O. SULZBERGER, JR.</u>

Dear Mr. Sulzberger

<u>The New York Times</u> front-page the "Pentagon Pinocchio's." In
addition, The Times ran an editorial on the gentlemen who have
overstated the Pentagon needs to Congress. Too, your newspaper ran
a revealing story on Prudential Securities and the problems of the
stockbrokers in that organization.

In <u>The New York Times</u> of July 5, 1993, page 2, you ran the enclosed
ad concerning <u>The New York Times</u>; on page 17 of the same paper,
you ran "Don't Miss A Beat..."; on page 10 in the same paper, you ran
another ad praising <u>The New York Times</u>; and on page 26 of the July
5, 1993 <u>New York Times</u>, you ran another ad telling us about <u>The New
York Times</u>.

Isn't there any room in <u>The New York Times</u> to tell the other side of the story concerning the treatment of, not only spasmodic dysphonia by Direct Voice Rehabilitation and the cures by Direct Voice Rehabilitation, a non-medical approach, but the story as well of President Clinton's hoarse voice and why it remains hoarse.

I'm just inquiring.

Mr. Wade of your science division says he will get back to me about running information concerning the problem of spasmodic dysphonia and a different view than the medics have. I believe that is what he had written to me, but my mind is getting fuzzy concerning what has been said and what has not been said.

Couldn't we just do a story about what is going on with spasmodic dysphonia and Bill Clinton's hoarse voice?

Incidentally, I love the blurbs you run about <u>The New York Times</u>. Occasionally, you miss a story and I believe the ones I have in mind are the ones you have overlooked.

I wouldn't miss your paper for the world, even though I am not in it.

With continued good cheer,

Most cordially,

Morton Cooper, Ph.D.

MC/anb
Enclosures

cc Jane Brody
   Nicholas Wade

MORTON COOPER, PH.D.

A Speech Pathology Corporation

VOICE REHABILITATION
SPEECH AND LANGUAGE THERAPY

Westwood Medical Plaza
10921 Wilshire Blvd. #401
LOS ANGELES, CALIFORNIA 90024
(310) 208-6047 208-6748
FAX (310) 208-8737

July 19, 1993

The New York Times
229 West 43rd Street
New York, NY 10036

ATTN: <u>ARTHUR O. SULZBERGER, JR.</u>

Dear Mr. Sulzberger

There were great stories on the front page of <u>The New York Times</u> dealing with air pollution contributing to asthma and perhaps 60,000 deaths a year from asthma and other respiratory diseases. Another story dealt with shock therapy — all well-balanced stories. In the Living Arts Section, the "Publisher Complains of Biased Bookstores..." and you had a well-balanced story on Erwin A. Glikes, the publisher of The Free Press.

I wonder, would it be possible to do a similar story on the treatment of hoarse voice and spasmodic dysphonia, as they are both tied together. Untold, countless millions suffer from hoarse voice and are treated medically, as is President Bill Clinton, and untold members suffer with the strangled voice — spasmodic dysphonia, are given poison and told there are no cures. There are cures for both the hoarse voice and the strangled voice.

Enclosed is an article I have just done for <u>Let's Live Magazine</u>. My study on hoarse voice was printed in the number one journal and indicates it has an excellent prognosis — cures by Direct Voice Rehabilitation, so, too, for the strangled voice.

I look forward to hearing from you in the near future.

Most cordially,

Morton Cooper, Ph.D.

MC/anb
Enclosures

cc Jane Brody
   Nicholas Wade

PS I have sent you a video of cured spasmodic dysphonia patients before, if you want another copy, please let me know.

MORTON COOPER, PH.D.
A Speech Pathology Corporation

VOICE REHABILITATION
SPEECH AND LANGUAGE THERAPY

Westwood Medical Plaza
10921 Wilshire Blvd. #401
LOS ANGELES, CALIFORNIA 90024
(310) 208-6047 208-6748
FAX (310) 208-8737

July 20, 1993

The New York Times
229 West 43rd Street
New York, NY 10036

ATTN: <u>ARTHUR O. SULZBERGER, JR.</u>

Dear Mr. Sulzberger

I love fashion just as much as anyone else and delight in seeing full-page ads in <u>The New York Times</u> such as page B-4 in the July 20, 1993 edition. I also am delighted to read of the screenwriter who found success in the last scene of the new Clint Eastwood movie. I am heartened by the story of Listening to the Patients' Emotional Needs in the section Science Times — all in the July 20, 1993 edition.

I am saddened to find that not only the pacific Voice Conference seems closed, but additional major meetings decline to allow cures of spasmodic dysphonia to be presented at these meetings. Medicine's position is Do No Harm, yet it administers poison, Botox, a sugar-coated term for Botulinum Toxin, to patients, now worldwide. Medicine's answer to spasmodic dysphonia is poison and the rage and fashion of poison declines to listen to or discuss cures by a non-medical, non-poison approach to spasmodic dysphonia. <u>The New York Times</u> prides itself in publishing all the news that's fit to print. Couldn't it find a reporter to investigate my inquiry and concern about medicine's one-sided approach to spasmodic dysphonia and also to President Clinton's hoarse voice — the medical treatment being change of diet, Zantac, for reflux, and allergy shots, all apparently to no avail as the President remains hoarse.

In previous correspondence of yesterday, I sent you my published study of hoarse voice done in 1974, with copies going to Jane Brody and your science editor, Mr. Wade. Isn't it fair that <u>The New York Times</u> afford its readership an alternative to medical intervention for hoarse voice and spasmodic dysphonia, an approach that has been reporting cures for years in the top journals?

As ever, I remain,

Most cordially,

Morton Cooper, Ph.D.

MC/anb
Enclosures

cc Jane Brody
   Nicholas Wade

MORTON COOPER, PH.D.
A Speech Pathology Corporation

VOICE REHABILITATION
SPEECH AND LANGUAGE THERAPY

Westwood Medical Plaza
10921 Wilshire Blvd. #401
LOS ANGELES, CALIFORNIA 90024
(310) 208-6047 208-6748
FAX (310) 208-8737

July 26, 1993

The New York Times
229 West 43rd Street
New York, NY 10036

ATTN: <u>ARTHUR O. SULZBERGER, JR.</u>

Dear Mr. Sulzberger

President Clinton was on the front page of <u>The New York Times</u> today, July 26, 1993, running. The President talks hoarse. There is not a word about his on-going hoarse voice that I find in <u>The New York Times</u>, correct me, if you will.

Isn't there room in <u>The New York Times</u> to provide for another view of President Clinton's hoarse voice than that of the medical one, namely, diet change, acid from the stomach to the vocal cords (reflux) and allergy? For years, I have helped thousands and thousands of people overcome their hoarse voices by Direct Voice Rehabilitation. Won't you allow me the opportunity to join with you so that when President Clinton runs, he can run with a clear efficient voice, and talk with one, as well.

I know <u>The New York Times</u> wants to publish all the news that's fit to print. I believe that helping people overcome hoarse voice is news that's fit to print.

With all good cheer,

Most cordially,

Morton Cooper, Ph.D.

MC/anb

cc Jane Brody
    Nicholas Wade, Science Editor

MORTON COOPER, PH.D.
A Speech Pathology Corporation

VOICE REHABILITATION
SPEECH AND LANGUAGE THERAPY

Westwood Medical Plaza
10921 Wilshire Blvd. #401
LOS ANGELES, CALIFORNIA 90024
(310) 208-6047 208-6748
FAX (310) 208-8737

August 18, 1993

The New York Times
229 West 43rd Street
New York, NY 10036

ATTN: <u>ARTHUR O. SULZBERGER, JR.</u>

Dear Mr. Sulzberger

As I have written in the past, <u>The New York Times</u> does marvelous, intriguing stories on a variety of topics, essentially getting to the essence directly, succinctly, and in highly readable fashion. Your newspaper covers every facet of life on the world, national, and local level, affording its readers a full and varied picture of the topic at hand. There is, however, one area that remains somewhat obscured in shadow and shrouded in mystery, and that is the area of voice. Our voice is very often our signature, a primary means of representing ourselves to the world, yet very little is known about it and when it becomes troublesome, interfering with our lives and our ability to communicate, we become frustrated at the lack of understanding by many of the people we expect to provide answers. The President of the United States, Bill Clinton, remains hoarse and is constantly hampered by a troubled voice, yet he has been following the medical model for some time, apparently, with little success, as becomes obvious to anyone who has heard him recently. Why? Ear-Nose-Throat doctors have basically 6 hours of training on the speaking voice, yet they are the ones the public flocks to when they begin to experience troubled voices. They have been cited time and again as authorities in Jane Brody's columns, yet they have very little training in the speaking voice and many themselves have poor voices. They are not trained in helping the speaking voice when it come to functional (non-organic) voice problems such as hoarse voice (without growths) such as Bill Clinton's hoarse voice. Too, medical people acknowledge their lack of training privately, but they keep this out of the public view.

I am not out to fault the medical people per se. There is a larger, more constructive agenda at hand. I ma simply trying to pint out that medical people do not have the training and background to make judgments and tell others, the public, and Jane Brody, what is right or wrong with the speaking voice, and all too often the singing voice as well, yet they are the ones running the show, treating the speaking and singing voice with medications, surgery, poison, etc. This leaves the patient open only to invasive procedures, which are merely palliative in nature and never touch the real problem of the voice itself.

The essence of my concern has always been the welfare of the patient, to see that he/she receives the best possible care and that can only happen when all the information is provided so that the patient is able to make a decision based on informed consent. The New York Times has, in the past, been a forum and provided a forum to those with ideas that may differ with the establishment, but whose knowledge is beneficial to its readership. I am asking The New York Times to continue with that policy and print an alternative view of treatment for voice problems. Now, especially, when we have a President who is suffering with a voice problem that he need not have, seems a most opportune time to tackle this little-known area and shed some much needed light onto a field that, in many ways, remains arcane in its views. I am asking The New York Times and Jane Brody to take another look at voice (including spasmodic dysphonia) with a fresh eye and perhaps give my views and my approach an airing so that people do not have to suffer with impaired voices or think that the only answer is an invasive approach. Isn't it time that <u>The New York Times</u> acknowledge my technique of Direct Voice Rehabilitation, a simple and natural approach with long-term results. I would be delighted to provide any information you may require for an in depth piece, including the names and phone numbers of patients who have been curd and recovered from all manner of voice problems, from the hoarse voice that Bill Clinton suffers from to the very severe condition of spasmodic dysphonia.

Please let me hear from you at your convenience.

Most cordially,

Morton Cooper, Ph.D.

MC/anb

MORTON COOPER, PH.D.
A Speech Pathology Corporation

VOICE REHABILITATION
SPEECH AND LANGUAGE THERAPY

Westwood Medical Plaza
10921 Wilshire Blvd. #401
LOS ANGELES, CALIFORNIA 90024
(310) 208-6047 208-6748
FAX (310) 208-8737

September 22, 1993

The New York Times
229 West 43rd Street
New York, NY 10036

ATTN: <u>JANE E. BRODY</u>

Dear Ms. Brody:

I have just completed a book titled, <u>You Are Losing Your Voice and
Don't Know It</u> and I would like you to comment on the on the sections
relating to <u>The New York Times</u>. I would appreciate your response to
the material that I will shortly send you.

I love the blurbs about <u>The New York Times</u>.

Most cordially,

Morton Cooper, Ph.D.

MC/anb
Enclosures

cc Arthur O. Sulzberger, Jr.

MORTON COOPER, PH.D.
A Speech Pathology Corporation

VOICE REHABILITATION
SPEECH AND LANGUAGE THERAPY

Westwood Medical Plaza
10921 Wilshire Blvd. #401
LOS ANGELES, CALIFORNIA 90024
(310) 208-6047 208-6748
FAX (310) 208-8737

September 22, 1993

The New York Times
229 West 43rd Street
New York, NY 10036

ATTN: <u>ARTHUR O. SULZBERGER, JR.</u>

Dear Mr. Sulzberger

I read that your cousin died recently. He was active and aware and lived a full life.

My condolences.

Most cordially,

Morton Cooper, Ph.D.

MC/anb

MORTON COOPER, PH.D.
A Speech Pathology Corporation

VOICE REHABILITATION
SPEECH AND LANGUAGE THERAPY

Westwood Medical Plaza
10921 Wilshire Blvd. #401
LOS ANGELES, CALIFORNIA 90024
(310) 208-6047 208-6748
FAX (310) 208-8737

October 8, 1993

Ms. Jane E. Brody
The New York Times
229 West 43rd Street
New York, New York 10036

Dear Ms. Brody

The flu season is upon us and all too often the speaking voice is affected, going hoarse. What about a column dedicated to "Laryngitis: The Voice That Came In From the Cold, How To Beat It If The Medical Help Doesn't Help."

Betty Rome, an attorney, experienced laryngitis during and after a cold. Medical help never helped her to regain her voice; in fact, the help she got resulted in bowed vocal cords. I estimate that 15-20% of all voice patients I see who suffer from voice problems began the problem due to a cold. I have been in practice over 30 years and I have seen well over 10,000 people who factualize this view.

The medical approach to hoarse or laryngitis — steam, humidifiers, bedrest, voice-rest, bed and voice-rest, antibiotics, steroids, do not help for a given percentage of cases that experience laryngitis.

Would you consider a column on how to self-help the laryngitic voice when medicine does not help by an alternative or combination to medicine such as Direct Voice Self-Help?

Looking forward to hearing from you.

Most cordially,

Morton Cooper, Ph.D.

MC/anb
Enclosures

MORTON COOPER, PH.D.
A Speech Pathology Corporation

VOICE REHABILITATION
SPEECH AND LANGUAGE THERAPY

Westwood Medical Plaza
10921 Wilshire Blvd. #401
LOS ANGELES, CALIFORNIA 90024
(310) 208-6047 208-6748
FAX (310) 208-8737

October 18, 1993

Nicholas Wade, Science Editor
THE NEW YORK TIMES
229 West 43rd Street
New York, New York 10036

Dear Mr. Wade:

The flu season is upon us and all too often the speaking voice is affected, going hoarse. What about a column dedicated to "Laryngitis: The Voice That Came In From the Cold, How To Beat It If The Medical Help Doesn't Help."

Betty Rome, an attorney, experienced laryngitis during and after a cold. Medical help never helped her to regain her voice; in fact, the help she got resulted in bowed vocal cords. I estimate that 15-20% of all voice patients I see who suffer from voice problems began the problem due to a cold. I have been in practice over 30 years and I have seen well over 10,000 people who factualize this view.

The medical approach to hoarse or laryngitis — steam, humidifiers, bed-rest, voice-rest, bed and voice-rest, antibiotics, steroids, do not help for a given percentage of cases that experience laryngitis.

Would you consider a column on how to self-help the laryngitic voice when medicine does not help by an alternative or combination to medicine such as Direct Voice Self-Help?

Looking forward to hearing from you.

Most cordially,

Morton Cooper, Ph.D.

MC/anb
Enclosures

MORTON COOPER, PH.D.
A Speech Pathology Corporation

VOICE REHABILITATION
SPEECH AND LANGUAGE THERAPY

Westwood Medical Plaza
10921 Wilshire Blvd. #401
LOS ANGELES, CALIFORNIA 90024
(310) 208-6047 208-6748
FAX (310) 208-8737

November 24, 1993

Jane E. Brody
The New York Times
229 West 43rd Street
New York, New York 10036

Dear Ms. Brody:

I was taken with your article today about anger. My recent book (see
enclosed) seems to touch on this area of anger. I hope that my book
is not counter-productive in that truth-telling is counter-productive.
Could you, would you, read my book and see if you become angry
about what is happening in the name of science and medicine in the
treatment of voice.

In the November 23, 1993 issue of <u>The New York Times</u>, you ran
an article headlined: "Her Study Shattered The Myth That Fraud In
Science Is a Rarity." Medicine's treatment of voice, especially Spasmodic
Dysphonia, might be labeled, "The Joys of Poison By Medicine for
Voice, Stuttering, and Now Facial Wrinkles, Brought to You By the
Kindly Folks at Columbia Presbyterian Hospital."

I don't have high blood pressure, I don't have anxiety, I just have a lot of anger and, as Neil Simon once said when asked about his anger, he replied that he had enough to start the Third World War by himself. I just have enough anger to write <u>Voice Suicide: The All-American Game, You're Losing Your Voice and You Don't Know It</u>. I believe writing a book is productive — not counter-productive, and I hope you will help me make my productive approach known to your readers. Spasmodic Dysphonia is curable by Direct Voice Rehabilitation and I have produced these cures for the past 20 years. Isn't it about time, Ms. Brody, to allow your readers to know there is an alternative to poison for Spasmodic Dysphonia?

Enclosed is an article from <u>ASHA</u>, a journal which I subscribe to and an organization I am a member of, which has ballyhooed surgery for 20 years and now says that 2/3 of the patients undergoing this procedure are worse off than before the surgical procedure. Now <u>ASHA</u> is endorsing poison and ignoring cures for Spasmodic Dysphonia by Direct Voice Rehabilitation. (see my book).

The picture alongside your article of someone purporting to be angry really doesn't do justice to my feelings of what anger is about.

I wonder, would you help me assuage my anger and tell about cures of Spasmodic Dysphonia by Direct Voice Rehabilitation (please see enclosed letters and article from <u>Cosmopolitan</u>.)

As you may notice in the <u>ASHA</u> article, "Let's Talk," they list sources for poison as you listed in your column Dr. Brin, who brings the joys of poison for Spasmodic Dysphonia. Could you not list a source who does not use poison for Spasmodic Dysphonia and presents cures by Direct Voice Rehabilitation. Whatever happened to medicine's Do No Harm and The New York Times' "All the news that's fit to print."?

Talk about anger; Ms. Brody, you ought to study me.

In closing, I have enjoyed the on-going pictures of various attire of models displaying the latest fashions. I love the ladies fashions, but isn't there some room, just a little room, in your newspapers, in your column, to talk about the joys of cures of Spasmodic Dysphonia and hoarse voice like the President of the United States endures, by my method of Direct Voice Rehabilitation.

Just asking.

Most cordially,

Morton Cooper, Ph.D.

MC/anb
Enclosures

cc Arthur O. Sulzberger, Jr.
   Nicholas Wade

MORTON COOPER, PH.D.
A Speech Pathology Corporation

VOICE REHABILITATION
SPEECH AND LANGUAGE THERAPY

Westwood Medical Plaza
10921 Wilshire Blvd. #401
LOS ANGELES, CALIFORNIA 90024
(310) 208-6047 208-6748
FAX (310) 208-8737

December 8, 1993

Mr. Arthur O. Sulzberger, Jr.
THE NEW YORK TIMES
229 West 43rd Street
New York, New York 10036

Dear Mr. Sulzberger

On December 7, 1993, on the fashion page, B-6, I was intrigued with the fashions presented to me. (Enclosed is a picture for your review and consideration.) On December 8, 1993, I was greeted on B-8 with the enclosed announcement: "Evolve Into a Higher Species."

I love fashion as well as anybody else, especially the ladies, sir, but isn't there just a little room in the Living Arts or Science Section to mention that there are cures of spastic dysphonia by Direct Voice Rehabilitation without poison or surgery? Couldn't we evolve into a higher species by and do no harm conservative approach to hopeless voices that are cured by Direct Voice Rehabilitation year after year?

Just asking?

With all good cheer.

Happy Chanukah and Merry Christmas and a Happy New Year.

Most cordially,

Morton Cooper, Ph.D.

MC/anb
Enclosures

MORTON COOPER, PH.D.
A Speech Pathology Corporation

VOICE REHABILITATION
SPEECH AND LANGUAGE THERAPY

Westwood Medical Plaza
10921 Wilshire Blvd. #401
LOS ANGELES, CALIFORNIA 90024
(310) 208-6047 208-6748
FAX (310) 208-8737

December 15, 1993

Mr. Arthur O. Sulzberger, Jr.
The New York Times
229 West 43rd Street
New York, New York 10036

Dear Mr. Sulzberger:

I know this may sound presumptuous of me and I hope you don't
take it as such, but would it be possible to have a personal face-to-face
meeting with you, Ms. Brody, and Mr. Wade to discuss our difference
so view concerning the treatment of spasmodic dysphonia. It seems to
me that it is more than just a matter of news but a matter of principle
as well as The New York Times prides itself on publishing all the news
that's fit to print, that possibly there is something to print about Direct
Voice Rehabilitation and the cures it presents for spasmodic dysphonia.

Just asking.

Most cordially,

Morton Cooper, Ph.D.

MC/anb

December 22, 1993

Morton Cooper, Ph.D.
Westwood Medical Plaza
10921 Wilshire Blvd. #401
Los Angeles, CA 90024

Dear Dr. Cooper:

Thank you for your letter to Arthur Sulzberger,Jr., to which he has asked me to reply.

Let me make the following points.

Jane Brody will next write about spasmodic dysphonia when it again comes into the news and not before. At that time she may or may not mention your work, depending on her and my judgment of its relevance to the news at hand.

It follows that there is nothing to be gained by your continuing to write letters to her, to me or to our publisher.

Could I therefore ask you, please, to drop this subject since there is no point in further discussion.

Yours sincerely,

Nicholas Wade

cc. Arthur Sulzberger,Jr.
    Jane Brody

MORTON COOPER, PH.D.
A Speech Pathology Corporation

VOICE REHABILITATION
SPEECH AND LANGUAGE THERAPY

Westwood Medical Plaza
10921 Wilshire Blvd. #401
LOS ANGELES, CALIFORNIA 90024
(310) 208-6047 208-6748
FAX (310) 208-8737

December 28, 1993

Nicholas Wade, Science Editor
THE NEW YORK TIMES
229 West 43rd Street
New York, New York 10036

Dear Mr. Wade:

The investigative stories by The New York Times in certain areas are so superb that I wonder why it leaves spastic/spasmodic dysphonia and treatment of this condition so on-sided, today Botox, yesterday surgery. The New York Times has on its masthead, "All The News That's Fit to Print." I gather cures and recoveries of spasmodic dysphonia by Direct Voice Rehabilitation does not enter that category.

As you know, I have sent you a copy of a forthcoming book that discusses at length my experience with the medical world and speech pathology in ignoring cures of spastic dysphonia by Direct Voice Rehabilitation. I will let the book address the issue of treatment of not only spastic dysphonia, but other voices in general, including President Bill Clinton's voice which remains hoarse.

In respect to your request that I cease and desist writing to Mr.

Sulzberger, Ms. Brody and to you, I will honor your request. I shall not cease in my efforts to bring a reasoned discussion of voice and spastic dysphonia and the treatment of such to the public.

With all good cheer.

Most cordially,

Morton Cooper, Ph.D.

MC/anb

cc Arthur O. Sulzberger, Jr.
    Jane Brody

LAWRENCE R. SPIRA, M.D.
TWO S. UNIVERSITY DRIVE
SUITE 110
PLANTATION, FLORIDA 33324

September 12, 1994

To Whom It May Concern:

During the late 1970's, I was diagnosed as having a sq. papilomma of the vocal cords. My speech was shot and for several years I had several surgeries all to no avail, talking caused pain and fatigue.

Eventually I saw Dr. Morton Cooper and even though I was suspect of his methods and frustrated, I retrained my speaking through his coaching and repetition. His method was difficult but as the months went on my speech became normal to this day in October, 1994. Even today occasionally when my voice becomes tired I go back to the old method AND in a day or two I'm once again okay, by practicing Dr. Cooper's methods.

Sincerely,

Lawrence R. Spira, M.D.

P.S. You have my full permission to use this statement and my case for full publication and disclosure. You may edit as needed. I sincerely hope this may help others who feel they have no way to a normal non-painful voice.

MORTON COOPER, PH.D.
A Speech Pathology Corporation

VOICE REHABILITATION
SPEECH AND LANGUAGE THERAPY

BRENTWOOD SQUARE
11661 SAN VICENTE BLVD. SUITE 301
LOS ANGELES, CALIFORNIA 90049
PHONE (310) 208-6047 FAX (310) 207-6769
E-MAIL: VOICEDOCTR@AOL.COM
WEBSITE: WWW.VOICE-DOCTOR.COM

February 28, 1995

Jane Brody
The New York Times
229 West 43rd Street
New York, New York 10036

Dear Ms. Brody:

A I am a subscriber to The New York Times, I found the enclosed article concerning the lack of solutions for problems by journalism of interest pertaining to spasmodic dysphonia.

Patients with spasmodic dysphonia lack options and alternatives to poisoned vocal cords and surgery for this condition, I find. Won't you afford these patients an opportunity to know there are cures and recoveries by my program of Direct Voice Rehabilitation in your column in an updated treatment of spasmodic dysphonia?

In letters to the NIH, Senator Tom Harkin, and Speaker Newt Gingrich, you might find my frustration at the media for not presenting cures and recoveries by a non-medical approach to spasmodic dysphonia. Forgive me, if I sound somewhat taken back by the adulation of surgery and poisons by medicine in the media. Perhaps, it would be helpful if you knew those touting Botulinum Toxin (Botox) in these newsletters proudly proclaim their frequent mentions in "Jane Brody's nationally syndicated Health Column..."

Please, please help tell the public and people suffering a so-called hopeless voice problem that there is hope and cures and recoveries by a program of Direct Voice Rehabilitation.

Most cordially,

Morton Cooper, Ph.D.

MC/anb
Enclosures

MORTON COOPER, PH.D.
A Speech Pathology Corporation

VOICE REHABILITATION
SPEECH AND LANGUAGE THERAPY

BRENTWOOD SQUARE
11661 SAN VICENTE BLVD. SUITE 301
LOS ANGELES, CALIFORNIA 90049
PHONE (310) 208-6047 FAX (310) 207-6769
E-MAIL: VOICEDOCTR@AOL.COM
WEBSITE: WWW.VOICE-DOCTOR.COM

November 22, 1996

Ms. Jane Brody
The New York Times
229 West 43rd Street
New York, NY 10036

Dear Ms. Brody:

I read your November 13, 1996 "Personal Health" column with great interest and want to compliment you on your balanced approach to alternative medicine. I was struck by the last two sentences in your column: "Do not assume that if it is 'natural' it is safe. Botulism toxin and hemlock are perfectly natural; they are also deadly."

Forgive me if I note the irony that you endorsed botulinum toxin as a treatment for spasmodic dysphonia in your March 11, 1992 column. Despite the enthusiasm of the medical community for this treatment, it is accurate to say that "normal or near-normal speech" is defined very generously by the proponents of botulinum toxin. The result is typically a weak and breathy voice, not a normal voice, and the improvement is short-term at best. Negative side effects have been reported in the literature, and the long-term effects of continued injections of this toxin are still unknown.

I urge you to familiarize yourself with non-invasive treatment alternatives, including Direct Voice Rehabilitation which is described in the enclosed book. The enclosed video will allow you to see and hear recoveries and cures through this technique for yourself.

Most cordially,

Morton Cooper, Ph.D.

MC/mhc
Enclosures

MORTON COOPER, PH.D.
A Speech Pathology Corporation

VOICE REHABILITATION
SPEECH AND LANGUAGE THERAPY

BRENTWOOD SQUARE
11661 SAN VICENTE BLVD. SUITE 301
LOS ANGELES, CALIFORNIA 90049
PHONE (310) 208-6047 FAX (310) 207-6769
E-MAIL: VOICEDOCTR@AOL.COM
WEBSITE: WWW.VOICE-DOCTOR.COM

June 11, 1997

Ms. Jane Brody
The New York Times
229 West 43rd Street
New York, New York 10036

Dear Ms. Brody:

What on Earth is going on?

You, Jane Brody reported the only way to treat Spasmodic Dysphonia
(SD), a term for strangled voices and throats, is medical intervention
with surgery or botulinium toxin, called Botox (*New York Times*,
Personal Health, March 11, 1992).

Not so, not so.

Medical Treatment doesn't have a single cure of SD that I know of
in over 125 years since it was described back in 1871 as "nervous
hoarseness" by Traube.

I report cures and recoveries of SD for 25 years by Direct Voice
Rehabilitation, a natural, non-invasive, non-medical approach.

Who has to know?

When you, Ms. Brody wrote the column on SD care, you weren't made aware of DVR and cures and recoveries of SD. Isn't there room for a pluralistic view of SD? One that reports cures and recoveries, documented, proven, by DVR from top medical centers, top medical doctors and top speech pathologists? (see "Reports of Cures and Recoveries From SD" enclosed).

The *NY Times* prides itself on printing all the news fit to print. I love the NY Times blurbs about extra terrestrials and what on earth is going on in the world: Giving SD patients an option and an alternative to surgery and poisoned vocal cords by DVR and a chance for cures and recoveries seems news fit to print.

Cordially,

Morton Cooper, Ph.D.

cc Arthur O. Sulzberger, Jr.
   Cory Dean

enclosures

MORTON COOPER, PH.D.
A Speech Pathology Corporation

VOICE REHABILITATION
SPEECH AND LANGUAGE THERAPY

BRENTWOOD SQUARE
11661 SAN VICENTE BLVD. SUITE 301
LOS ANGELES, CALIFORNIA 90049
PHONE (310) 208-6047 FAX (310) 207-6769
E-MAIL: VOICEDOCTR@AOL.COM
WEBSITE: WWW.VOICE-DOCTOR.COM

June 18, 1997

Ms. Jane Brody
The New York Times
229 West 43rd Street
New York, New York 10036

<u>CORRECTED COPY</u>

Dear Ms. Brody:

I have recently seen a spasmodic dysphonia patient treated with botulinum toxin who reports severe negative effects from this substance. I am enclosing the letter of Jean Long because her doctor was Doctor Brin. He was one of the sources for your column that espoused botulinum toxin as the treatment of choice for spasmodic dysphonia. I asked that the letter from this patient not be used (save for documentation purposes). This patient's reaction is not singular. Additional patients, a schoolteacher treated with botulinum toxin reported that her tongue and lips curled after a second botox shot. She asked the doctor if the problem could have come from the botox. She reports his answer was that it was from her developing dystonia problem. This patient was treated by Dr. Mitchell Brin. An assistant U.S. Attorney, a Federal Prosecutor, was seen in my office because a second botox shot left him with a frightening voice and a severe breathing problem.

It is said that botulinum toxin or botox is safe and effective in the short-run.

I am prepared at your request to provide documentation for these cases.

Enclosed is a two page response I've made to those who believe strangled voices are hopeless. In your column, dated March 11, 1992, you indicate that the medical approach (surgery or botulinum toxin) is the sole answer to spasmodic dysphonia (strangled voices).

For the patients' sake, I hope you will update your column to give hope to hopeless voices and allow cures and recoveries from troubled and strangled voices by DVR (Direct Voice Rehabilitation) as an option for voice-troubled patients.

Most cordially,

Morton Cooper, Ph.D.

cc Arthur O. Sulzberger, Jr.
   Cory Dean

MC/js

MORTON COOPER, PH.D.

A Speech Pathology Corporation

VOICE REHABILITATION
SPEECH AND LANGUAGE THERAPY

BRENTWOOD SQUARE
11661 SAN VICENTE BLVD. SUITE 301
LOS ANGELES, CALIFORNIA 90049
PHONE (310) 208-6047 FAX (310) 207-6769
E-MAIL: VOICEDOCTR@AOL.COM
WEBSITE: WWW.VOICE-DOCTOR.COM

July 15, 1997

Ms. Jane Brody
The New York Times
229 West 43rd Street
New York, NY 10036

Ms. Brody:

The case I'm discussing in this paragraph is not an isolated one. An Assistant U.S. Attorney, a Federal Prosecutor named Duro Duplechin had a second Botox shot that left him unable to talk and breathe. The U.S. Government referred this patient to my office for intense Direct Voice Rehabilitation (DVR) as I am the only one who reports cures and recoveries of Spasmodic Dysphonia.

Another patient, a school teacher reports after a second Botox shot that her lips and tongue curled and was told that the Botox shot was not responsible. "It was the dystonia", she was told that was creating the problem.

Jean Long, an SD patient details her experience with the negative effects of Botox. She had severe body rashes. Her hair was falling out as well as her nails. See enclosed letter.

The Assistant U.S. Attorney has gone public to discuss his problem and has given up the right of privacy and confidentiality as does Jean Long. I use their names to document the negative side-effects of Botulinum Toxin. I ask that you not use their names for other than documentation.

Countless patients of mine with SD who have been seen by neurologists report they do not have any neurological symptoms other than SD. The medical community relates SD as a dystonia. Suggested areas have been the central nervous system and today especially the basal ganglia of the brain. On autopsy, I understand there is no difference found in the brain of an SD patient and a normal person.

SD was initially said to be due to "a mind problem". For fifty to sixty years psychiatrists probed the mind of patients with SD. Not a single cure has been recorded that I know of. Surgery came next and for approximately twenty years dominated the field of Spasmodic Dysphonia. Not a single cure that I know of was reported in the countless articles that were peer-reviewed and said to be the state of the art and treatment of choice. The surgical procedure has been phased out by the medical community and replaced by Botulinum Toxin, one of the world's deadliest poisons as the state-of-the art and treatment of choice. Not a single cure has been reported that I know of in the literature. In fact the medical community says there are no cures of this condition. The American Speech and Hearing Association reports that there are no cures of this condition.

Medicine says that Botulinum Toxin (Botox) is safe and effective in the short-run. The three opening paragraph of this letter to you indicate that this is not so. In the long-run, medicine acknowledges that it doesn't know the long-term, downside effects of Botulinum Toxin on the body. As you know, the FDA has not approved Botulinum Toxin for Spasmodic Dysphonia.

My central thesis and concern is that patients with Spasmodic Dysphonia as well as other troubled voices are basically not given an option to medical intervention. Direct Voice Rehabilitation is proven successful for almost all types of voice disorders over the past thirty years. See my enclosed bibliography. Direct Voice Rehabilitation is safe and effective, not only for Spasmodic Dysphonia but for all types of voice disorders. Direct Voice Rehabilitation may be a state-of-art and a treatment of informed choice for patients with SD and voice problems.

Medicine and the American Speech and Hearing Association say the patients welfare comes first. If so, then informed choice and consent must be a prerequisite for any approach to SD or voice disorders. I believe that medicine ignores this dictum in favor of a one-sided approach called Botulinum Toxin for SD and medical intervention as well for troubled voices.

Your column is dedicated to health. I ask that you afford your readers the opportunity to understand there is a different approach to voice health for voice problems and especially SD. I have reported cures and recoveries of SD for the past 25 years by DVR. I ask that you allow your readers to realize there is hope for hopeless voices such as SD and troubled voices in general. My view of troubled voices is that 25% of our population suffer them. There are simple, natural, direct ways to often self-help our voices. Won't you allow your column and your readers to be privy to such an alternative approach than medical intervention alone? I hope you do not take the position that your mind is made up and you do not want to be troubled by facts.

Most cordially,

Morton Cooper, Ph.D.

cc: Arthur O. Sulzberger, Jr.
     Cory Dean

MORTON COOPER, PH.D.
A Speech Pathology Corporation

VOICE REHABILITATION
SPEECH AND LANGUAGE THERAPY

BRENTWOOD SQUARE
11661 SAN VICENTE BLVD. SUITE 301
LOS ANGELES, CALIFORNIA 90049
PHONE (310) 208-6047 FAX (310) 207-6769
E-MAIL: VOICEDOCTR@AOL.COM
WEBSITE: WWW.VOICE-DOCTOR.COM

August 12, 1997

Cory Dean
Science Editor
The New York Times
229 West 43rd Street
New York, NY 10036

Dear Ms. Dean:

Here are cures and recoveries from Spasmodic Dysphonia, before and after presentations from top medical doctors and medical centers.

Most cordially,

Morton Cooper, Ph.D.

Enclosure
MC/js

MORTON COOPER, PH.D.
A Speech Pathology Corporation

VOICE REHABILITATION
SPEECH AND LANGUAGE THERAPY

BRENTWOOD SQUARE
11661 SAN VICENTE BLVD. SUITE 301
LOS ANGELES, CALIFORNIA 90049
PHONE (310) 208-6047 FAX (310) 207-6769
E-MAIL: VOICEDOCTR@AOL.COM
WEBSITE: WWW.VOICE-DOCTOR.COM

August 13, 1997

Ms. Cory Dean
Science Editor
The New York Times
229 West 43rd Street
New York, NY 10036

Dear Ms. Dean:

In talking to the FBI Agents at the YMCA about Spasmodic Dysphonia
(SD)—
I work out there and they too, they reminded me that the FBI and
New York Times employees were given physical examinations by a fake
doctor. You do recall this situation. I am sure the FBI and New York
Times were very thorough in checking out this doctor in the beginning.
But in the end, they found they were wrong.

SD is neither neurological nor medical in nature, I find. I change
the SD voice in my office to a clear voice. If SD was neurological, a
dystonia (involuntary), a new voice voluntarily couldn't happen. Won't
you afford your readers, whether in the Brody column or elsewhere,
there is a non-medical way — DVR, Direct Voice Rehabilitation that
has been proven to be successful.

Cordially yours,

Morton Cooper, Ph.D.

Enclosures

cc: Arthur O. Sulzberger, Jr.
MC/js

MORTON COOPER, PH.D.
A Speech Pathology Corporation

VOICE REHABILITATION
SPEECH AND LANGUAGE THERAPY

BRENTWOOD SQUARE
11661 SAN VICENTE BLVD. SUITE 301
LOS ANGELES, CALIFORNIA 90049
PHONE (310) 208-6047 FAX (310) 207-6769
E-MAIL: VOICEDOCTR@AOL.COM
WEBSITE: WWW.VOICE-DOCTOR.COM

July 31, 1998

Ms. Jane E. Brody, Health Writer
The New York Times
229 West 43rd Street
New York, NY 10036

Dear Ms. Brody:

The advertisements for the New York Times on television and in your newspaper tells the reader to *"expect the world."*

Additionally, advertisements indicate, *"We look at the world for more perspectives, with more depth and breadth, to enrich your world, your many worlds, every single day."* Lately, heard on television is *"A world of understanding that others miss, The New York Times. Expect the world."*

Other ads such as the *"Extra Terrestrial — Extra coverage of the earth. And beyond."* Among the many others, one stands out: *"Ideas catch fire."*

Would it be possible to have balance in the treatment of SD? Ms. Brody says there is no other approach to the hopeless voice problem, except Botulinum Toxin-Botox and/or surgery.

It isn't true. I'm enclosing some literature for your review and consideration. Hopefully, the enclosed will cause you to reconsider your opinion.

Most cordially,

Morton Cooper, Ph.D.

MC:ma

cc: Arthur Sulzberger, Jr.
    Cory Dean
    Dr. Altman

MORTON COOPER, PH.D.
A Speech Pathology Corporation

VOICE REHABILITATION
SPEECH AND LANGUAGE THERAPY

BRENTWOOD SQUARE
11661 SAN VICENTE BLVD. SUITE 301
LOS ANGELES, CALIFORNIA 90049
PHONE (310) 208-6047 FAX (310) 207-6769
E-MAIL: VOICEDOCTR@AOL.COM
WEBSITE: WWW.VOICE-DOCTOR.COM

August 4, 1998

Ms. Jane E. Brody, Health Writer
The New York Times
229 West 43rd Street
New York, NY 10036

RE: Additional Advertisements — *"Informers"*

Dear Ms. Brody:

While pursuing the New York Times, I came upon another advertisement, *"Informers"*.

Would it be possible to *"Inform"* your readers that there is an alternative approach to the treatment of SD? An effective treatment which does not use Botulinum Toxin — Botox and/or surgery.

Being *"Informed"* requires being aware of your choices.

Most cordially,

Morton Cooper, Ph.D.

MC:ma

cc: Arthur Sulzberger, Jr.
    Cory Dean
    R. Altman

MORTON COOPER, PH.D.
A Speech Pathology Corporation

VOICE REHABILITATION
SPEECH AND LANGUAGE THERAPY

BRENTWOOD SQUARE
11661 SAN VICENTE BLVD. SUITE 301
LOS ANGELES, CALIFORNIA 90049
PHONE (310) 208-6047 FAX (310) 207-6769
E-MAIL: VOICEDOCTR@AOL.COM
WEBSITE: WWW.VOICE-DOCTOR.COM

February 12, 1998

<u>REPORTS OF CURES, RECOVERIES, AND IMPROVEMENTS FROM SPASMODIC AND SPASTIC DYSPHONIA (SD) BY DIRECT VOICE REHABILITATION (DVR)</u>

Spastic Dysphonia and Spasmodic Dysphonia (SD) are among the most debilitating of all voice disorders. The condition of a strangled, strained voice was first described in 1871 by Traube. SD is considered incurable by traditional medicine, by the National Spasmodic Dysphonia Association, and by the American-Speech-Language-Hearing Association.

The current treatment for SD is injections of a substance called botulinium toxin (Botox) or surgery. In 1991, at Irvine, CA, at a major meeting on SD, a leading medical doctor, fearing the long-term effects of Botox, asked that this treatment be withdrawn at the earlier possible time in favor of another substance. Some serious negative effects following the use of Botox have been reported by some patients (documentation on file), and negative aspects of Botox, including the need for repeated injections (possibly for life), are of concern.

My approach to these so-called "hopeless" voice disorder is changing the voice through Direct Voice Rehabilitation (DVR). For the past twenty-five years, I have successfully treated patients with these conditions; from my experience, SD is caused by voice misuse and abuse, not by neurological factors.

In 1982, at Cedars-Sinai Medical Hospital, I presented patients with confirmed severe SD who told of recovering their speaking voices by DVR. The late Henry J. Rubin, a well-known ENT specialist, asked during the presentation: "We know that you are the only one successful by speech therapy. Why?" The answer is, "I do not do speech therapy; I do Direct Voice Rehabilitation." In 1990, Dr. Rubin commented: "In the fifteen years immediately preceding my retirement from the active practice of otolaryngology, I have referred my patients in need of voice rehabilitation to Dr. Cooper because his results proved to be the most consistently satisfactory. His methods seemed essentially to be quite simple, in fact to the point sometimes of challenging believability, but they worked. He explains these methods in his book, and I believe that any voice therapist who gives them a serious and unbiased trial will be agreeably surprised." In 1993 he wrote to me: "The medical and speech professions may continue to deny your obvious successes, but it is because of unfamiliarity with what you actually do. Ignorance of your methods breeds fear, and that equates with resistance and denial."

The cures, recoveries, or improvements of SD patients diagnosed by the following doctors and medical centers have been amply documented: Paul Ward, M.D., Gerald S. Berke, M.D., Edward A. Kantor, M.D., Robert Feder, M.D., Sam Pearlman, M.D., and Henry J. Rubin, M.D., UCLA Medical Center, Head and Neck Division; Robert W. Bastian, M.D., Department of Otolaryngology, Loyola University Chicago; Hans V. von Leden, M.D., Head and Neck Division, USC Medical Center, to mention a few.

Dr. Gerald Berke referred Mrs. Gayle Pace, who was diagnosed with Adductor and Abductor Spastic Dysphonia. Mrs. Pace was returned to UCLA Medical Center with a normal voice within one month of a program of DVR. She remains cured of SD approximately five years after treatment. Another of Dr. Berke's SD patient's sought a non-medical approach. After short term therapy, the patient recovered 95% of her normal voice and remains excellent one year following the conclusion of therapy. Dr. Berke referred the Reverend Henry Sellers, with a diagnosis of SD, to my office for DVR; this patient, still in therapy, has substantially recovered a normal voice. Rabbi Alan Green, diagnosed with Adductor SD at UCLA Medical Center, undertook my program of DVR; he reports he is cured of the problem and does not think of his voice anymore.

Dr. Edward A. Kantor diagnosed two cases of Adductor SD; both patients have remained cured for approximately ten years following DVR. Dr. Kantor said: "Dr. Morton Cooper has shown unusual expertise in treating patients with spastic dysphonia. His methods of voice therapy in our patients afflicted with this markedly disabling disease have been highly successful."

Dr. Paul Ward diagnosed Mrs. Marjorie Whitman as having severe SD. After undergoing my program of Direct Voice Rehabilitation, this patient was returned to Dr. Ward at UCLA, and the recovery of the normal voice was confirmed.

Dr. Arnold Aronson of the Mayo Clinic diagnosed the Reverend James Johnson with a severe case of Adductor Spastic Dysphonia, which he had had for eight years. The Reverend Johnson has been cured for eleven years following the completion of DVR.

In 1974 Dr. Hans V. von Leden diagnosed Professor T. as having SD, referring this patient to me. The professor reports he has a normal voice since completing therapy in 1975. Another of Dr. von Leden's patients, a lawyer diagnosed with SD, reports that he has been cured for the past twelve years.

Dr. Robert W. Bastian diagnosed Abductor Spasmodic Dysphonia in two patients who were seen for one month of intensive DVR. Both report the recovering of a normal voice.

These are but a few cases that I cite to indicate successes of SD of all types by DVR. I am grateful to my patients for permission to release their names and/or files to document and confirm cures, recoveries, and/or improvements from SD by DVR. I am also grateful to the doctors who have availed themselves of my services to assist their patients by DVR.

In this day and age with various forms of "alternative medicine" being recognized and practiced by the medical profession, I believe that any patient who has been diagnosed with SD, suspected SD or any other voice disorder should be appraised of Direct Voice Rehabilitation as a potential and possible cure, recovery or improvement, especially since treatment is non-invasive, and dramatic results may be observed after a brief period of treatment. DVR can be replicated by other voice pathologists.

In 1973, in my voice pathology text, entitled <u>Modern Techniques of Vocal Rehabilitation</u>, I wrote of cures, recoveries, and improvements from SD by DVR. In 1980, I presented a paper "Recovery from Spastic Dysphonia by Direct Voice Rehabilitation" at the 18th Congress of the International Association of Logopedics and Phoniatrics. I have written chapters for professional handbooks and have published in medical/scientific journals on voice and voice disorders. My experience includes being on the Staff and Faculty of UCLA Medical Center, Head and Neck Division, serving as Director of its Voice and Speech Clinic.

Chapters from my latest book, <u>Stop Committing Voice Suicide</u>, on SD and other troubled voices, are on my Web site (http://www.voice-doctor.com). Articles on SD and DVR are also on the web. My e-mail address is: VOICEDOCTR@aol.com.

For those interested in the cures, recoveries, and/or improvements of SD by DVR, an audio and a video of my SD patients before and after DVR are available.

This handout is intended to provide meaningful information for educated judgment regarding SD and other troubled voices using DVR. I welcome your views and comments.

Most cordially,

Morton Cooper, Ph.D.

MORTON COOPER, PH.D.
A Speech Pathology Corporation

VOICE REHABILITATION
SPEECH AND LANGUAGE THERAPY

BRENTWOOD SQUARE
11661 SAN VICENTE BLVD. SUITE 301
LOS ANGELES, CALIFORNIA 90049
PHONE (310) 208-6047 FAX (310) 207-6769
E-MAIL: VOICEDOCTR@AOL.COM
WEBSITE: WWW.VOICE-DOCTOR.COM

August 25, 1999

Ms. Jane E. Brody, Health Writer
The New York Times
229 West 43rd Street
New York, NY 10036

Ms. Brody,

In your column on Personal Health Tuesday, August 24th page D7, you indicate... "But no matter how grave the situation, a patient should never be told that 'nothing more can be done.' There is always something the doctor can offer. If there is no treatment that can curb the disease, there is at least treatment to make the patient as comfortable as possible. But the doctor should never suggest that palliative treatment might cure the disease and should make sure the patient understands that."

Additionally..... "When patients cannot be cured, feelings of guilt and helplessness may prompt the doctor to abandon the patient. An understanding word from the patient's family may help the doctor overcome these feelings and remain a source of comfort and hope. In dealing with bad news, doctors need all the help they can get."

I am enclosing statements by patients who have suffered from
Spasmodic Dysphonia. By a process of Direct Voice Rehabilitation they
can talk normally again. I've been reporting cures of this problem for
over 25 years.

In your article dated Wednesday, March 11, 1992 you indicate that
Spasmodic Dysphonia cannot be cured and only surgery or Botox is a
possible approach. Isn't it possible Ms. Brody, that you let your readers
know there is a non-medical approach, Direct Voice Rehabilitation
by me, that has been confirmed and proven to work for Spasmodic
Dysphonia? Won't you let me help patients know that there is an
alternative approach to Spasmodic Dysphonia, non-medical, that they
may consider if they have Spasmodic Dysphonia despite Diane Rehm's
statement on Ted Koppel's Nightline recently that there are no cures of
her condition? Wouldn't it be of relevance to let her know there is?

Most cordially,

Morton Cooper, Ph.D.

MC/aa
enclosure

MORTON COOPER, PH.D.
A Speech Pathology Corporation

VOICE REHABILITATION
SPEECH AND LANGUAGE THERAPY

BRENTWOOD SQUARE
11661 SAN VICENTE BLVD. SUITE 301
LOS ANGELES, CALIFORNIA 90049
PHONE (310) 208-6047 FAX (310) 207-6769
E-MAIL: VOICEDOCTR@AOL.COM
WEBSITE: WWW.VOICE-DOCTOR.COM

September 9, 1999

Ms. Jane E. Brody, Health Writer
The New York Times
229 West 43rd Street
New York, NY 10036

Ms. Brody,

Dr. James Suen, President Clinton's ENT wrote about *Stop Committing Voice Suicide* "it is constructive criticism." He has allowed us to put his comment about my book on my website.

Professor Johnson, of Utah University has indicated my view on spasmodic dysphonia and voice problems is a positive contribution to voice rehabilitation (see enclosed letter).

Your article on tea is helpful. I wonder if you'd be kind enough to amend your position on the treatment of spasmodic dysphonia to include non-medical intervention by Direct Voice Rehabilitation. Enclosed are letters from Ginger Chang and Sylvia Cheek that have just come in.

Nobody gets a story right 100% of the time Ms. Brody. I'm not asking you to correct the story on Spasmodic Dysphonia. I'm asking you to add on another approach, an option to those who don't find help with botulinum toxin (Botox), or surgery... or who do not want an invasive procedure and prefer Direct Voice Rehabilitation.

Can't you find it within your province to afford your readers the option of Direct Voice Rehabilitation for Spasmodic Dysphonia and other bad voices?

Most cordially,

Morton Cooper, Ph.D.

MC/aa
enclosure

MORTON COOPER, PH.D.
A Speech Pathology Corporation

VOICE REHABILITATION
SPEECH AND LANGUAGE THERAPY

BRENTWOOD SQUARE
11661 SAN VICENTE BLVD. SUITE 301
LOS ANGELES, CALIFORNIA 90049
PHONE (310) 208-6047 FAX (310) 207-6769
E-MAIL: VOICEDOCTR@AOL.COM
WEBSITE: WWW.VOICE-DOCTOR.COM

March 28, 2000

Ms. Jane Brody

RE: Balanced spasmodic dysphonia position

The New York Times
229 West 43rd Street
New York, NY 10036
Ms. Brody,

Your article in the Tuesday, March 28th, Science Section of The New York Times gives hope to those with cancer. Your comment "...many doctors initially consulted by cancer patients are not up on the latest and most effective treatments for their disease." That statement is apropos for spasmodic dysphonia as well.

I continue to report cures and recoveries and improvements of spasmodic dysphonia by a simple process called Direct Voice Rehabilitation.

You headline one of the paragraphs **HOW TO BECOME A WINNER.** You quote a father of a cancer patient who states in the film Cancer: Evolution to Revolution: "The care you get is largely dependent on you."

It would be decent of you to afford your readers the option of Direct Voice Rehabilitation which reports cures of a so-called hopeless voice problem, spasmodic dysphonia, in contrast to the position that you remain with that there are no cures of spasmodic dysphonia.

In the December, 1999 National Spasmodic Dysphonia Association Newsletter, page 7, Dr. Gerald Berke, Chairman of UCLA Head and Neck Division reports regarding Botox (botulinum toxin): "...there are some obvious drawbacks. It requires lifelong visits from 4 to 10 times per year for repeat injections. The injections are not inexpensive. The interval between post injection breathiness, good voice, and the return of symptoms may not be very long in some patients. Hypersensitivity and antibody formation have been shown to produce some long term structural changes in muscle cells."

Surgery and Botox have never reported a single cure of spasmodic dysphonia. Medical treatment has never reported a single cure of spasmodic dysphonia since 1871. Direct Voice Rehabilitation reports ongoing cures since 1973. Isn't it appropriate that you allow your readers to know that there is a conservative non-invasive procedure that has been curing spasmodic dysphonia for over 25 years?

Most cordially,

Morton Cooper, Ph.D.

MC/aa
enclosure

MORTON COOPER, PH.D.
A Speech Pathology Corporation

VOICE REHABILITATION
SPEECH AND LANGUAGE THERAPY

BRENTWOOD SQUARE
11661 SAN VICENTE BLVD. SUITE 301
LOS ANGELES, CALIFORNIA 90049
PHONE (310) 208-6047 FAX (310) 207-6769
E-MAIL: VOICEDOCTR@AOL.COM
WEBSITE: WWW.VOICE-DOCTOR.COM

April 5, 2000

RE: Second Opinion

Ms. Jane E. Brody
Health Writer
The New York Times
229 West 43rd Street
New York, NY 10036

Ms. Brody,

A second opinion for biopsies is relevant and valuable according to the Tuesday, April 4, 2000 Health and Fitness article. Another article in the *New York Times* by Abigail Zuger, M.D., says expect a chill asking for a second opinion in the examining room. Both articles indicate a second opinion is appropriate and relevant.

Would it be possible for you to afford your readers suffering from Spasmodic Dysphonia a second opinion regarding treatment. The medical position and the National Spasmodic Dysphonia Association believe that spasmodic dysphonia is hopeless and look to surgery and botulinum toxin (Botox). Patients suffering with spasmodic dysphonia or any condition should get a second opinion on treatment. Could you not afford your readers such a second opinion and consider Direct Voice Rehabilitation for spasmodic dysphonia in your column?

Most cordially,

Morton Cooper, Ph.D.

MC/aa

MORTON COOPER, PH.D.
A Speech Pathology Corporation

VOICE REHABILITATION
SPEECH AND LANGUAGE THERAPY

BRENTWOOD SQUARE
11661 SAN VICENTE BLVD. SUITE 301
LOS ANGELES, CALIFORNIA 90049
PHONE (310) 208-6047 FAX (310) 207-6769
E-MAIL: VOICEDOCTR@AOL.COM
WEBSITE: WWW.VOICE-DOCTOR.COM

December 5, 2001

Mr. Arthur Sulzberger, Sr.
Mr. Arthur Sulzberger, Jr., Publisher
The New York Times
229 West 43rd Street
New York, NY 10036

Mr. Sulzberger,

Over the years I've written to you, to Ms. Brody, to those associated with the *NY Times* Science Section, to the editor Joseph Lelyveld, now replaced by Mr. Boyd asking that you review your position on the treatment of Spasmodic Dysphonia (SD), the strangled voice. Ms. Brody wrote almost 10 years ago that the only treatment for this condition is Botox, a deadly poison or surgery. One of the sources that provided background for Ms. Brody's position that there are no cures of this problem, SD was Mitchell Brin, M.D. Dr. Brin has moved over to the Allergan corporation that produces Botox as a top executive for that corporation.

Ms. Brody writes well but in the column enclosed she was given limited information. Your son, Arthur Sulzberger, Jr., was recently on Brian Lamb's interview C-Span this past week indicating that the *NY Times* does make mistakes but looks to rectify them. I hope that you would afford readers of the *NY Times* the privilege of knowing that there is another approach to the treatment of SD other than Botox and surgery. Neither approach reports a single cure ever by medical intervention.

Medical treatment has failed to provide a cure since Traube first described the condition in 1871. The medical paradigm for SD believes the condition is a Dystonia. Hopeless for a cure. My paradigm for SD is the condition is due to bad use of the voice (see enclosed cures in CSHA). My approach (DVR) validates my non-medical paradigm with cures for over 25 years.

Why write to you now? Jane Brody writes on December 4, 2001, page D7, the headline is Needless Silence for Hearing Impaired. At the end of her column she affords several websites for further guidance. Very decent. In the column she wrote almost 10 years ago, which I am enclosing for you, she gave no choice for treatment other than medical intervention for SD considered to be hopeless. I have been reporting cures of this condition by a process called Direct Voice Rehabilitation (DVR) for over 30 years. The cases are documented, not anecdotal, and substantiated by long-term follow-ups that the cures are lasting.

I ask the *NY Times* to allow choice of treatment for the condition known as SD thereby affording patients an opportunity to decide for themselves what treatment they might seek. Appropriate treatment can be afforded any patient, not only those suffering SD, when they have full disclosure to make a wise decision of what might be appropriate care for them.

Am I asking too much of the *NY Times*? I ask that you afford your readers the opportunity to look at my web and to read my material not exclusively but in conjunction with the material that they may be presented by medical sources.

The National Spasmodic Dysphonia Association (NSDA) which is a mainstay for information for those suffering SD is given a generous donation of money over the years by Allergan, the maker of Botox.

The NSDA is a non-profit organization but it seems to me to be quite partisan in presenting medical treatment for SD and ignoring non-medical care by DVR. I am enclosing statements that have been reported in the California Speech-Language-Hearing Association and at the Pacific Voice Conference to give you a sense of my position on the treatment of SD hoping that in keeping with the *NY Times* dictum that informed readers are good citizens and informed patients can make appropriate choice.

Will you consider a wider scope of treatment for SD patients? Many SD patients endure terrible mental and physical trauma suffering SD. These patients are given no hope for a cure, and suffer ongoing Botox shots, 4 o 10 a year or more, or surgery, that does not address the basic cause of SD, misuse and abuse of the voice.

Most cordially,

Morton Cooper, Ph.D.

MC/aa

Subj: **No Subject**
Date: Monday, April 22, 2002 1:09:04 PM
From: publisher@nytimes.com
To: VOICEDOCTR@aol.com

Thank you for your e-mail. Due to the volume, I cannot promise to answer
every e-mail sent. But I do promise to read every one.   Arthur
Sulzberger Jr.

———————— Headers ————————
Return-Path: <publisher@nytimes.com>
Received: from rly-xi02.mx.aol.com (rly-xi02.mail.aol.com [172.20.116.7]) by air-xi03.mail.aol.com
(v84.14) with ESMTP id MAILINXI31-0422160904; Mon, 22 Apr 2002 16:09:04 -0400
Received: from gatekeeper2.nytimes.com ([199.181.175.211]) by rly-xi02.mx.aol.com (v84.15) with
ESMTP id MAILRELAYINXI21-0422160900; Mon, 22 Apr 2002 16:09:00 -0400
Received: from mailhub1.nytimes.com (mailhub1.nytimes.com [170.149.204.38])
    by gatekeeper2.nytimes.com (Switch-2.2.1/Switch-2.2.0) with ESMTP id g3MK7wi17250
    for <VOICEDOCTR@aol.com>; Mon, 22 Apr 2002 16:07:59 -0400 (EDT)
Received: from nyt-notes-01.nytimes.com (nyt-notes-01.nytimes.com [170.149.63.169])
    by mailhub1.nytimes.com (Switch-2.2.1/Switch-2.2.0) with ESMTP id g3MK7PI29623
    for <VOICEDOCTR@aol.com>; Mon, 22 Apr 2002 16:07:25 -0400 (EDT)
X-Priority: 3 (Normal)
From: "Publisher/CORPHQ/NYTIMES" <publisher@nytimes.com>
To: VOICEDOCTR@aol.com
Message-ID: <OF85256BA3.006A8694-ON85256BA3.006A8694@nytimes.com>
Date: Mon, 22 Apr 2002 15:23:32 -0400
X-MIMETrack: Serialize by Router on NYT-Notes-01/NYT/NYTIMES(Release 5.0.8 |June 18, 2001
 04/22/2002 03:53:09 PM
MIME-Version: 1.0
Content-type: text/plain; charset=us-ascii

Subj: **re: NY Times**
Date: Tuesday, April 23, 2002 12:48:30 PM
From:
To: publisher@nytimes.com, managing-editor@nytimes.com

Mr. Sulzberger,

I have corresponded with you over the years asking that you correct the Jane E. Brody misleading and false representation that she unknowingly and unintentionally presented in a column concerning the treatment of Spasmodic Dysphonia (SD). I write to you on behalf of the millions of people who suffer SD and who are given no hope for a cure and no choice for treatment save Botox and/or surgery. Neither of which has ever reported a single cure. The medical treatment of SD has never had a single cure for over 130 years Mr. Sulzberger. Is it not time for you to intervene and address the endorsement by Jane E. Brody's prestigious column that there is no hope and no cure for SD in the very face of ongoing cures by me for over 30 years? Is there no sense of fair play and balanced reportage on SD at the *NY Times*? Your newspaper, which I read and admire, carries the logo "All the news fit to print." Are not cures of a hopeless voice problem ongoing for over 30 years proven and confirmed news fit to print in the *NY Times*?

I recently saw you on television interviewed by Brian Lamb. You said you look to balanced reporting. I was stirred by your commentary. I fear though that your commentary is simply rhetoric. Am I wrong?

Botox has become the number one treatment for SD. The surgical procedure that Jane E. Brody recommended in her column has been relegated to the dustbin of history according to the *Journal of Voice Editor* Robert Sataloff, M.D. In the name of medicine, we are poisoning the vocal cords with four to ten injections of Botox or more a year, each and every year for life. And nobody knows the long-term downside effects of the body.

Dr. Mitchell Brin who was a source for Jane E. Brody telling her of Botox for SD is now an executive with the Allergan Company. Dr. Brin was the one who brought Botox to the field of SD treatment. In 1991, Dr. Brin said at the Pacific Voice Conference, held in Irvine California at 3:00pm on March 10, 1991 before hundreds of people including medical people and speech pathologists as well as patients suffering SD that he wanted to withdraw Botox at the earliest possible time in favor of another substance fearing the long-term downside effects of the body by Botox. That statement disappeared from the radar screen, publications and discussion and the video that was to be made available concerning the presentation but was never made available. Doesn't this information warrant concern and interest on the part of the *NY Times*, Mr. Sulzberger? Doesn't the reporting of names of SD patients diagnosed by top medical doctors in the country and cured of a so-called hopeless voice problem by a non-medical program interest you sufficiently to do a story of another approach to SD than the one Jane E. Brody has allowed to stand and remain a form of disinformation and a disservice to the medical community, to SD patients, and to *NY Times* readers?

Most cordially,

Morton Cooper, Ph.D.

Subj: **No Subject**
Date: Tuesday, April 23, 2002 12:54:20 PM
From: publisher@nytimes.com
To: VOICEDOCTR@aol.com

Thank you for your e-mail. Due to the volume, I cannot promise to answer
every e-mail sent. But I do promise to read every one.   Arthur
Sulzberger Jr.

———————————— Headers ————————————
Return-Path: <publisher@nytimes.com>
Received: from rly-xb02.mx.aol.com (rly-xb02.mail.aol.com [172.20.105.103]) by air-
xb05.mail.aol.com (v84.10) with ESMTP id MAILINXB54-0423155420; Tue, 23 Apr 2002 15:54:20
0400
Received: from gatekeeper1.nytimes.com ([199.181.175.210]) by rly-xb02.mx.aol.com (v84.10) w
ESMTP id MAILRELAYINXB210-0423155404; Tue, 23 Apr 2002 15:54:04 -0400
Received: from mailhub2.nytimes.com (mailhub2.nytimes.com [170.149.204.40])
    by gatekeeper1.nytimes.com (Switch-2.2.1/Switch-2.2.0) with ESMTP id g3NJs3O23741
    for <VOICEDOCTR@aol.com>; Tue, 23 Apr 2002 15:54:03 -0400 (EDT)
Received: from nyt-notes-01.nytimes.com (nyt-notes-01.nytimes.com [170.149.63.169])
    by mailhub2.nytimes.com (Switch-2.2.1/Switch-2.2.0) with ESMTP id g3NJrvr29641
    for <VOICEDOCTR@aol.com>; Tue, 23 Apr 2002 15:53:57 -0400 (EDT)
X-Priority: 3 (Normal)
From: "Publisher/CORPHQ/NYTIMES" <publisher@nytimes.com>
To: VOICEDOCTR@aol.com
Message-ID: <OF85256BA4.006CFF8C-ON85256BA4.006CFF8C@nytimes.com>
Date: Tue, 23 Apr 2002 15:50:33 -0400
X-MIMETrack: Serialize by Router on NYT-Notes-01/NYT/NYTIMES(Release 5.0.8 |June 18, 2001
 04/23/2002 03:38:18 PM
MIME-Version: 1.0
Content-type: text/plain; charset=us-ascii

Subj: **Cures of Spasmodic Dysphonia**

Date: Wednesday, August 14, 2002 12:08:15 PM

From:

To: executive-editor@nytimes.com

Mr. Howell Raines
Executive Director
NY Times
229 West 43rd Street
New York, NY 10038

Mr. Raines,

I am a voice and speech doctor. I report cures of hopeless voices called Spasmodic Dysphonia (SD). In popular terms it's called the strangled voice. I've been reporting cures of this hopeless voice condition for over 30 years. Why am I writing to you? The California Speech-Language-Hearing Association (CSHA) has banned my cures and information regarding choice of treatment for this condition. President Lisa O'Connor of this organization has banned the ads on the basis they challenge the failed theories of medicine that have not one single cure in 130 years since Traube first described the condition in 1871. She bans choice of treatment by banning the ads I have run.

Your health columnist Jane E. Brody in 1992 I believe did a column of the treatment of SD. She was touted by Mitchell Brin, M.D. that only Botox and/or surgery was the treatment of choice. He informed her there are no cures of this condition. That surgery is now considered to be in the dustbin of history by Robert Sataloff, M.D. and Editor of the Journal of Voice. In my three ads that I'm sending you, I indicate that Botox as with surgery is failing in its treatment of SD. Botox and surgery and other medical treatments as I noted earlier in this letter have never had one single cure of SD.

Brody is not interested in updating her column and your Science editor is not interested in presenting a different picture on the treatment of SD. Are you?

Incidentally my ads reporting cures of SD have been banned in the American Speech-Language-Hearing Journal, The Journal of Voice, and The Annals of Otology, Rhinology and Laryngology (see enclosure).

Most cordially,

Morton Cooper, Ph.D.

MORTON COOPER, PH.D.
A Speech Pathology Corporation

VOICE REHABILITATION
SPEECH AND LANGUAGE THERAPY

BRENTWOOD SQUARE
11661 SAN VICENTE BLVD. SUITE 301
LOS ANGELES, CALIFORNIA 90049
PHONE (310) 208-6047 FAX (310) 207-6769
E-MAIL: VOICEDOCTR@AOL.COM
WEBSITE: WWW.VOICE-DOCTOR.COM

March 6, 2003

RE: Botox for spastic vocal cords

New York Times
229 West 43rd Street
New York, NY 10038

Letter to the Editor,

The Sunday, March 2, 2003 front page of the *New York Times* article on Botox says that Botox gives "patients with spastic vocal cords back their voices." The spastic vocal cords are called Spasmodic Dysphonia (SD). Dr. Herb Dedo, a famed ENT at The Medical Center at the University of California, San Francisco has characterized Botox for the spastic vocal cords (SD) as a roller coaster ride. The vocal cord recovery is iffy, temporary at best. Breathy or whisper voice, some voice or hoarse voice for a short while, then more spasms and spastic vocal cords are back. Patients suffering spastic vocal cords and the strangle strain voice are not told of the possible serious consequences of Botox on the vocal cords and their health. Bo for botulinum and tox for toxin. It may not be user friendly for all too many.

**in the December, 1999 National Spasmodic Dysphonia Association

<u>Newsletter</u>, page 7, Dr. Gerald Berke, Chairman of UCLA Head and Neck Division reports regarding Botox (botulinum toxin): "...there are some obvious drawbacks. It requires lifelong visits from 4 to 10 times per year for repeat injections. The injections are not inexpensive. The interval between post injection breathiness, good voice, and the return of symptoms may not be very long in some patients. Hypersensitivity and antibody formation have been shown to produce some long term structural changes in muscle cells." Botox for spastic vocal cords doesn't seem to me or the patients I see and hear from providing the vocal cord recovery.

My simple approach of Direct Voice Rehabilitation (DVR) has lasting ongoing cures of Spasmodic Dysphonia for over thirty years. The cures were noted in academic and scientific publications.

Medicine hasn't had one single cure of spastic vocal cords (SD whether by Botox or surgery) since Traube first described Spasmodic Dysphonia back in 1871.

Perhaps it is time to allow spastic vocal cord talking patients and those suffering like voice problems the knowledge that they don't have hopeless voice problems but are simply using a wrong voice which medical people and my colleagues aren't aware of.

If you check my website (www.voice-doctor.com), you will find a huge printout on cures of Spasmodic Dysphonia, reportage of cures at major medical centers and medical meetings.

I am Dr. Morton Cooper, formerly Director of The Voice and Speech Clinic, UCLA Medical Center as well as Assistant Clinical Professor, Head and Neck Division, Department of Surgery, UCLA Medical Center. I have been in private practice in West Los Angeles for over thirty years.

Most cordially,

Morton Cooper, Ph.D.

June 24, 2003

Sherri Fox
Editor
ADVANCE

RE: Spasmodic Dysphonia: Current Treatment and Research

Andrew Blitzer, MD, and Christy Ludlow, Ph.D. are of the view that SD is a neurological problem. Andrew Blitzer, MD states: "Current methods are treating the symptoms, not the disorder. Botox is the best symptomatic treatment we have at this moment until we are able to manipulate the brain." (NSDA Newsletter Vol. 12 No. 2 Oct. 2003)

Christy Ludlow, Ph.D. states: "It's going to be extremely important to look at central abnormalities. Focusing on the neuropathology of people who have had spasmodic dysphonia will be critical." (NSDA Newsletter Vol. 12 No. 2 Oct. 2003)

With all deference to their expertise, it may appear that spasmodic dysphonia is not a neurological problem, but in reality a voice problem without any neurological involvement.

Those suffering from Spasmodic Dysphonia (SD) should know that there is hope for a cure, as my work in the past demonstrates. For over thirty years, I have reported, and continue to report ongoing cures by a process called DVR, Direct Voice Rehabilitation.

The medical field, ASHA, and associated organizations though well intended tell us SD is hopeless, beyond a cure. I have reported some thirty cures of SD by DVR, and many more recoveries and improvements. That means that I have taken the time to follow them up sufficiently to establish that SD is curable, and that the cure is lasting.

SD is caused by the use of the wrong voice. It requires a change of voice and often a change of breathing support. Most importantly, it also requires a change of self-image, of voice image, a psychological attribute which takes real work to understand and overcome. Not everyone is able to overcome their voice image. Nor are all those who recover their voice able to maintain it, almost invariably for the lack of attention to right practice.

I ask those who suffer SD to believe that it is not a medical condition, bit a misphonia, a wrong use of voice, which is unintentionally and unknowingly established. Its impact is devastating. Some give up and take their own lives, while others become hermits or recluses, not realizing that SD is amendable to a cure through a change of voice. With competent direction, we can get out of the abyss that is SD.

My message is: Change Your Voice, Change Your Life. You can, if you understand what is happening to your voice, and if you are willing to give up a wrong voice in favor of a right one.

The essence of the matter is that SD is not a dystonia, but rather a misphonia. Already back in 1973, I characterized it as a mechanical problem when I wrote my textbook, *Modern Techniques of Vocal Rehabilitation*. That means that we, you and I, were doing something wrong in the use of our voices and didn't know it. But, with expert direction we can know better and change if we have the mindset to do so, and if we devote the time and effort to change a wrong voice to a right voice.

That is why I wrote two other books, *Change Your Voice, Change Your Life* and *Stop Committing Voice Suicide*. We are the victims of wrong voice use and don't know it.

I also published my cures and recoveries from SD in a peer-reviewed report in the *International Association of Logopedics and Phoniatry* in 1980.

The medical folks look at SD and associated voice problems as medical in nature, and treat them with Botox, surgery, and drugs, including reflux drugs, etc. If you find the help you want there, fine. However, if you don't find the help you want through medical intervention, don't give up. There is light at the end of the tunnel.

In 1991, a leading ENT doctor was asked before an audience of about five hundred people at the Pacific Voice Conference, if there were a light at the end of the tunnel for those suffering SD. "No," she replied, "there is no light at the end of the tunnel."

At the 1998 Pacific Voice Conference I was allowed to present cures of SD by DVR. I presented cures of people who had been diagnosed with the most severe SD by the UCLA Medical Center's Head and Neck Division, considered then and now as one of the foremost hospitals and medical centers in the world. The SD diagnoses were made by some of the Medical Center's Head and Division's top physicians, including Dr. Paul Ward, ENT, who was the chairman of the Medical Center's Head and Neck Division preceding the present chairman, Dr. Gerald Berke. For instance, Berke diagnosed Gayle Pace as having Adductor/Abductor SD. She was cured under my care by DVR. Pace remains cured of SD twelve years after my program of DVR. Ward diagnosed Marjorie Whitman with SD so severe, Dr. Ward recommended surgery. Whitman declined. She recovered a normal voice by DVR. Dr. Berke later diagnosed Rev. Henry Sellers as having a focal laryngeal dystonia. Rev. Sellers was also cured and remains cured by DVR. Dr. Berke diagnosed SD for Robert Peyton. Botox was advised. Peyton opted for DVR and is cured of SD.

The litany of cures by DVR is extensive. It includes Rev. James Johnson, diagnosed by the Mayo Clinic's Dr. Arnold Aronson as having very severe SD. Rev. Johnson was told to have surgery. He declined, tried an intensive one-month program of DVR, and still remains cured of SD over 17 years later.

There are other cures by my program of DVR, for those whom other ENTs associated with the UCLA Medical Center Head and Neck Division had diagnosed as SD. These ENTs and their patients include: Dr. Hans Von Leden, ENT: Professor T., plus another patient cured of SD by DVR, 30 & 15 years respectively.

Dr. HJ Rubin, ENT: four cases, all cured by DVR over a period of years.

Dr. Robert Feder, ENT: one case, cured, with the cure still remaining over twenty-plus years later.

Dr. Ed Kantor ENT: two cases, whose cures have now lasted over fifteen and twenty-plus years .

Additionally, I had the case of an ENT faculty professor at UCLA Medical Center whose wife was diagnosed with SD. She was referred to my private practice, choosing to ignore the option of surgery, which prevailed then, she was cured by DVR.

With these dramatic cures, and since SD is ostensibly incurable, some have asked, "Well, did these people really have SD?" I can only say that the top ENTs at UCLA Medical Center, "the beat in the west", diagnosed the SD cases I worked on in my private practice. There is no doubt: these people had SD. Furthermore, I have the audio and videos to prove that, indeed, SD is SD.

This trend of diagnosis with SD by the UCLA Medical Center, and cure by DVR, continues into the present. Dr. Gerald Berke, the present Chair of the Head and Neck Division at UCLA Medical Center is known as one of the best in his field. He has no cures of SD through medicine, either by surgery or by Botox. Indeed, those doing Botox or surgery are told SD is beyond a cure. Yet, the ENTs of UCLA Head and Neck Division have diagnosed a number of cases with SD, and I have helped their SD patients find a cure by DVR in my private practice.

Other documented and lasting cures and successes of SD by my DVR program include:

*Over two years ago, the Scripps Clinic in La Jolla diagnosed Ginger Chang, a young lady in her 20's, with Spasmodic Dysphonia. She was told that her condition was hopeless and that she required a lifelong series of Botox shots. After one week of my intensive program of Direct Voice Rehabilitation (30 hrs.), Ms. Chang found a normal and effective voice and has remained cured of her SD.

*Some 17 years ago, Dr. Arnold Aronson at the Mayo Clinic diagnosed extremely severe SD for the Rev. James Johnson. He was advised to have surgery; he declined. The Rev. Johnson underwent an intensive program of DVR with me for one month. He has remained cured of his problem for 17 years.

These are just a few of many documented and lasting cures and successes of SD by my DVR program.

In addition to the partial list of cures, there are numbers of recoveries and improvements from SD by DVR. Dan Hooyer, for instance, tried one Botox shot and gave it up; he then had 95% recovery by DVR. A medical doctor declined Botox and/or surgery, and achieved an 85% recovery by DVR. The list goes on.

At the present time Dr. Gerald Berke of UCLA Head and Neck Division is in charge and responsible for administering Botox injections to patients diagnosed with SD.

Denise Proudfoot was diagnosed by Dr. Berke as having SD and received four Botox shots from him. She declined further shots, underwent a program of DVR with me, and stated on TV, and in print, that she had achieved a 95% recovery from SD within a short period of time in my office. Ira Newborn was diagnosed by Dr. Berke with SD and was Botoxed. He had a voice that was frightening after the Botox shot. He actually had three different voices: One was a "Darth Vader-like" strangled voice, the second a falsetto, the third was one that "yodeled" uncontrollably between the two others. He received a half dose of Botox in mid-December 2002 and started DVR approximately three or four weeks later, while still suffering under the initial effects of the Botox. Even while affected by the Botox, he was able to recognize his true voice in seconds by DVR. Despite the severity of his voice problem, I was able to help him find and use a normal voice, which he characterizes as 85% at this time and continuing to improve.

My message on SD is simply this: It is not a hopeless voice problem. Whatever else we might believe about SD, one thing is clear: SD is curable by DVR. If you suffer from SD, you have the choice to treat it through DVR, rather than surgery and/or Botox injections.

May the gods be with you.

Most cordially,

Morton Cooper, Ph.D.
voicedoctr@aol.com

The New York Times

229 WEST 43rd STREET
NEW YORK, N.Y. 10036

DATE: _July 8_

FAX NUMBER: _310 207 6769_

TO: _Morton Cooper_

FROM: _Donald McNeil_

To: Morton Cooper —
I hope this helps.
Donald McNeil

All Databases   PubMed   Nucleotide   Protein   Genome   Structure   OMIM   PMC   Journals   Books

Search PubMed ⬍ for _________________________________   Go | Clear | Advanced Search

Limits   Preview/Index   History   Clipboard   Details

Display AbstractPlus   ⬍ Show 20 ⬍ Sort By ⬍ Send to ⬍

All: 1   Review: 0

1: Ann Otol Rhinol Laryngol. 2002 Jun;111(6):500-6.

Electrically stimulated glottal opening combined with adductor muscle botox blockade restores both ventilation and voice in a patient with bilateral laryngeal paralysis.

Zealear DL, Billante CR, Courey MS, Sant'Anna GD, Netterville JL.

Department of Otolaryngology--Head and Neck Surgery, Vanderbilt University Medical School, Nashville, Tennessee 37232, USA.

The purpose of this study was to determine whether paced electrical stimulation of the posterior cricoarytenoid muscle with an implantable device could restore ventilation in a patient with bilateral vocal fold paralysis without disturbing voice. In the first US case of a multi-institutional study, this patient was implanted with an Itrel II stimulator (Medtronic, Inc). In monthly postoperative sessions over an 18-month period, an effective stimulus paradigm was derived, the magnitude of stimulated vocal fold abduction and ventilation was measured, and perceptual judgments of voice quality were made. After identification of optimum parameters, posterior cricoarytenoid muscle stimulation produced a moderately large vocal fold abduction of 4 mm, but only marginal improvement in mouth ventilation, with no change in voice quality. After adductor muscle blockade with botulinum toxin, the patient's voice improved with increased phonatory airflow, but ventilation through the passive airway was still inadequate. However, by combining these two therapeutic strategies, dynamic abduction increased to 7 mm, ventilation through the mouth surpassed that through the tracheotomy (allowing decannulation), and voice quality was restored to normal.

PMID: 12090705 [PubMed - indexed for MEDLINE]

Related Articles

Effect of chronic electrical stimulation of laryngeal muscle on voice.

Reanimation of the paralyzed human larynx with an implantable electrical stimulation device.

Review Voice therapy for vocal fold paralysis. [Am. 2004]

Determination of the optimal conditions for laryngeal pacing with the Itrel II implantable stimulator.

Increased stability of airflow following botulinum toxin injection.

» See Reviews. | » See All

Display AbstractPlus   ⬍ Show 20 ⬍ Sort By ⬍ Send to ⬍

MORTON COOPER, PH.D.
A Speech Pathology Corporation

VOICE REHABILITATION
SPEECH AND LANGUAGE THERAPY

BRENTWOOD SQUARE
11661 SAN VICENTE BLVD. SUITE 301
LOS ANGELES, CALIFORNIA 90049
PHONE (310) 208-6047 FAX (310) 207-6769
E-MAIL: VOICEDOCTR@AOL.COM
WEBSITE: WWW.VOICE-DOCTOR.COM

March 2, 2005

Ms. Jane E. Brody, Health Writer
New York Times
229 West 43rd Street
New York, NY 10038

Ms. Brody,

You write about resiliency and cite a couple of books on that topic. You talk about your own health problems, and talk about your resiliency. May I ask you to consider your position on Spasmodic Dysphonia (SD)? And you resiliency to deny cures of it?

You indicate it's never to late to get with resiliency. How about allowing patients who suffer SD to know there are cures of the condition by what I do, Direct Voice Rehabilitation? Enclosed is a printout of just some of the cures I have achieved of SD. I'm sorry that I'm the only one in the world reporting cures for over 35 years. Maybe you could cite my book *Stop Committing Voice Suicide*, which addresses cures of SD? You list other books on resiliency and perhaps I would qualify as one who is resilient above adversity to report ongoing cures of SD.

Most cordially,

Morton Cooper, Ph.D.

MC/aa
Enclosure

MORTON COOPER, PH.D.
A Speech Pathology Corporation

VOICE REHABILITATION
SPEECH AND LANGUAGE THERAPY

BRENTWOOD SQUARE
11661 SAN VICENTE BLVD. SUITE 301
LOS ANGELES, CALIFORNIA 90049
PHONE (310) 208-6047 FAX (310) 207-6769
E-MAIL: VOICEDOCTR@AOL.COM
WEBSITE: WWW.VOICE-DOCTOR.COM

March 9, 2005

Ms. Jane E. Brody, Health Writer

RE: "Undertreated pain destroys lives."

New York Times
229 West 43rd Street
New York, NY 10038

Ms. Brody,

In regard to your March 8, 2005 personal health column titled, "A Fight for Full Disclosure of the Possible Pain": You seem extremely troubled by the severe pain you experienced following your knee replacements.

You come down to earth from your high ivory tower writing about sanitizing pain felt by Spasmodic Dysphonia (SD) patients and ignoring cures of this condition by my Direct Voice Rehabilitation (DVR) program. I quote you, "This is outrageous, and just reveals the monetary motives behind much of modern medicine. The patient be damned; just bring in the bucks." You are referring to your knee replacement medical care. It is apropos to SD, too.

You finally did get help for your pain and you could walk half a mile to your local Y and resume your daily swim. You state, "Undertreated pain destroys lives." You quote additionally an email message to you, "Unless you're the one feeling it, it's basically meaningless."

You push Botox the deadliest poison in the world that allows Allergan and the medical community to give four to ten Botox shots a year or more each and every year for life. Medicine guarantees that there are no cures for Spasmodic Dysphonia (SD) by Botox. You can assign the SD patients to a living hell Ms. Brody. You can assign them to a rollercoaster ride when they get a Botox shot and endure in and out voices with iffy outcomes and at times terrible results. You talk about your pain and ignore the pain of those you consign to a living hell. You leave those with SD with no choice of treatment save ongoing Botulism Toxin called Botox at a cost of $1000 or $2000 or $3000 per Botox shot. You carry the imprimatur of the *NY Times* behind you so that those suffering SD do not believe there could be a cure of SD in the face of my ongoing cures for over thirty-five years of SD.

You have joined the real world Brody when you talk about your pain. What about joining the real world and helping those with SD to have choice of treatment for SD? I enclose a brief summation of cures that provide evidence based research that name names of doctors and patients and medical centers that provide ongoing cures of SD. You and the *NY Times* decline to accept non-medical cures of SD. The *Science Times* is rife with only MDs reporting.

Yet the *NY Times* does a big spread on Hans Bethe, a Ph.D. who is a fantastic mind with fantastic discoveries and contributions to society, but you disallow Ph.D. types into the *Science Times*. What an oxymoron.

On March 2, 2003 the *NY Times* front-paged Botox as giving those with spastic vocal cords back their voices. This statement is such a terrible unqualified sham it is rather unbecoming of the *NY Times*. The *NY Times* remains a believer in the medical model, in medical treatment, and in medical failure for SD despite the fact that the medical profession has never reported a single cure of SD since Traube first described the condition in 1871.

When it comes to your pain Ms. Brody, you scream bloody murder. When it comes to the pain of others you write blightly about poisoning their vocal cords because it is in keeping with the medical profession adheres to and endorses when they are on the wrong road to the treatment of SD for over 130 years.

Pain, ah sweet pain, Ms. Brody, when it strikes you all hell breaks lose.

Most cordially yours,

Morton Cooper, Ph.D.

MC/aa
Enclosures

MORTON COOPER, PH.D.
A Speech Pathology Corporation

VOICE REHABILITATION
SPEECH AND LANGUAGE THERAPY

BRENTWOOD SQUARE
11661 SAN VICENTE BLVD. SUITE 301
LOS ANGELES, CALIFORNIA 90049
PHONE (310) 208-6047 FAX (310) 207-6769
E-MAIL: VOICEDOCTR@AOL.COM
WEBSITE: WWW.VOICE-DOCTOR.COM

March 10, 2005

RE: Jane E. Brody denies cures of hopeless voices called Spasmodic Dysphonia

Bill Keller
Executive Editor
New York Times
229 West 43rd Street
New York, NY 10038

Mr. Keller,

An editorial in the *NY Times* today March 3, 2005 was headlined "Looking the Other Way." The headline is apropos for the *NY Times* position on a condition called Spasmodic Dysphonia (SD). I am the only Doctor in the world reporting cures of SD. If you or your staff would check my website you will see that I have evidence based research to verify that I'm the only Doctor in the world reporting cures of this so-called hopeless voice problem. Jane E. Brody of your Personal Health Section Wednesday, March 11, 1992 wrote that there are no cures of SD. She got her information from Mitchell Brin, a neurologist who assured her that there are no cures of SD. That is Dr. Brin's view. He brought Botox to the field for SD in 1984. He was Jane E. Brody's source for her column saying that there are no cures of SD. Dr Brin knows better than all that. In 1991 at a meeting in Irvine, CA, March 2 at 3:00 pm before hundreds of people Dr. Brin asked that Botox be withdrawn at the earliest possible time fearing the long-term effects on the body. He is a Vice-President of Allergan now. Dr. Brin knows of my cures of SD as I presented in 1991 cures of SD at the same meeting that he asked that Botox be withdrawn for SD. As a Vice-President of Allergan he is of the view that his 1991 statement in 2003 is "dated".

Would you be interested in a story of why one lone Doctor reports cures of SD when all medicine and a drug company such as Allergan does not? The *NY Times* has fully endorsed Botox for SD and never mentioned cures of SD on its front-page March 2, 2003 article. This front-page March 2, 2003 position reported Botox is giving those with spastic vocal cords back their voices. The Botox voice? The Botox voice four to ten times a year or more each and every year for life. Jane E. Brody refuses to acknowledge my track record of ongoing cures of SD. The *NY Times* correspondence with the Sulzberger's on down including Nick Wade, Corey Dean, and others take the same position as Brody ignoring cures of SD.

Enclosed is just a partial listing of cures of patients with SD by me.

I have tried to contact Dan Oakrent the Ombudsman with the *NY Times* but he will not respond to my inquiry about the *NY Times* looking the other way on cures of SD. Will you?

Most cordially,

Morton Cooper, Ph.D.

MC/aa

MORTON COOPER, PH.D.
A Speech Pathology Corporation

VOICE REHABILITATION
SPEECH AND LANGUAGE THERAPY

BRENTWOOD SQUARE
11661 SAN VICENTE BLVD. SUITE 301
LOS ANGELES, CALIFORNIA 90049
PHONE (310) 208-6047 FAX (310) 207-6769
E-MAIL: VOICEDOCTR@AOL.COM
WEBSITE: WWW.VOICE-DOCTOR.COM

March 29, 2005

RE: Jane E. Brody denies cures of hopeless voices called Spasmodic Dysphonia

Bill Keller
Executive Editor
New York Times
229 West 43rd Street
New York, NY 10038

Mr. Keller,

I wrote to you directly recently but have not been greeted with a response you have received my concern about Spasmodic Dysphonia concerning the *NY Times* on that subject. Therefore I am sending my inquiry to you again certified. I simply would like to know: A) have you received my inquiry B) Received it but are not inclined to respond C) not received my inquiry and have no awareness of what I am writing or talking about D) don't care about Spasmodic Dysphonia, my inquiry and the subject?

This is a multiple answer response. Please be kind enough to check your response. Or, E) you don't care to respond to those who question the

NY Times or it's editors?

Most cordially,

Morton Cooper, Ph.D.

MC/aa

MORTON COOPER, PH.D.
A Speech Pathology Corporation

VOICE REHABILITATION
SPEECH AND LANGUAGE THERAPY

BRENTWOOD SQUARE
11661 SAN VICENTE BLVD. SUITE 301
LOS ANGELES, CALIFORNIA 90049
PHONE (310) 208-6047 FAX (310) 207-6769
E-MAIL: VOICEDOCTR@AOL.COM
WEBSITE: WWW.VOICE-DOCTOR.COM

March 31, 2005

Bill Keller
Executive Editor
New York Times
229 West 43rd Street
New York, NY 10038

Mr. Keller,

The *NY Times* on March 2, 2003 unequivocally endorsed Botox for Spasmodic Dysphonia (SD) reporting that Botox is giving those with spastic vocal cords back their voices. This was on the Sunday front-page edition if the *NY Times*. That story has no legs in the sense it has no documentation to bear out its position. The story was written by Douglas G. McNeil, Jr. who forwarded me the "documentation" which lacked documentation for the statement run in the story.

I've asked for a review of this story and a counter to it that reports cures of SD by what I do called Direct Voice Rehabilitation (DVR). I don't ask you to run a counter story to your front-page Botox endorsement for SD. I simply ask you to look into the fact that there are cures of SD and have been for 35 years by me. Botox has no cures.

In your March 30, 2005 Wednesday *NY Times* front-page bottom section, left, you investigated the medical advisor for baseball and found that he exaggerated his credentials. Very interesting story. It is the same story for Allergan the maker of Botox overreaching on the front-page of the *NY Times*, March 2, 2003. Is there no desire at the *NY Times* to look into its wholehearted endorsement of Botox for SD ignoring cures of SD and not providing choice of treatment for those who have SD and those who provide treatment for SD?

Most cordially,

Morton Cooper, Ph.D.

MC/aa

MORTON COOPER, PH.D.
A Speech Pathology Corporation

VOICE REHABILITATION
SPEECH AND LANGUAGE THERAPY

BRENTWOOD SQUARE
11661 SAN VICENTE BLVD. SUITE 301
LOS ANGELES, CALIFORNIA 90049
PHONE (310) 208-6047 FAX (310) 207-6769
E-MAIL: VOICEDOCTR@AOL.COM
WEBSITE: WWW.VOICE-DOCTOR.COM

April 13, 2005

Mr. Bill Keller
Executive Editor
New York Times
229 West 43rd Street
New York, NY 10038

Mr. Keller,

There seems to be a disconnect the editorial page of the *New York Times* and its reporting of the news. Today Wednesday April 13, 2005 your lead editorial is headlined Questioning Mr. Bolton. It is an excellent summary of the C-Span senate hearing on Mr. Bolton's nomination for the post of United Nations ambassadorship. I watched the entire hearing of Mr. Bolton. I believe he will be approved despite some deep concerns about his management style.

I have written to you and to the Sulzberger's, to former editors of the *New York Times*, to question the *New York Times* position on Spasmodic Dysphonia (SD). Apparently the *New York Times* will not question Jane E. Brody's column that says SD is incurable. As I noted in an earlier letter to you this week, the *New York Times* on its front page of March 2, 2003, ignored cures of SD and simply made the unqualified statement, without documentation that Botox is giving back those with spastic vocal cords their voices.

Nobody at the *New York Times* seems interested in exploring the simple fact that SD is curable, that SD is not a medical problem, and that cures of SD by non-medical help called Direct Voice Rehabilitation is a dirty word.

I don't understand why there is such a disconnect between the editorial page and the news coverage in the *New York Times* dealing with SD.

Most cordially,

Morton Cooper, Ph.D.

MC/aa
Enclosures

MORTON COOPER, PH.D.
A Speech Pathology Corporation

VOICE REHABILITATION
SPEECH AND LANGUAGE THERAPY

BRENTWOOD SQUARE
11661 SAN VICENTE BLVD. SUITE 301
LOS ANGELES, CALIFORNIA 90049
PHONE (310) 208-6047 FAX (310) 207-6769
E-MAIL: VOICEDOCTR@AOL.COM
WEBSITE: WWW.VOICE-DOCTOR.COM

April 13, 2005

Ms. Cornelia Dean
Science Times
New York Times
229 West 43rd Street
New York, NY 10038

Ms. Dean,

I was quite delighted to see that the Science Times is concerned with and interviewing those who are outstanding in their contributions to medicine but are not medics. Your medical writers for this section are excellent. But as your Op-Ed page runs columns with different views, I am now pleased to read not just medical columns but Ph.D. columns as well.

Most cordially,

Morton Cooper, Ph.D.

MC/aa

MORTON COOPER, PH.D.

A Speech Pathology Corporation

VOICE REHABILITATION
SPEECH AND LANGUAGE THERAPY

BRENTWOOD SQUARE
11661 SAN VICENTE BLVD. SUITE 301
LOS ANGELES, CALIFORNIA 90049
PHONE (310) 208-6047 FAX (310) 207-6769
E-MAIL: VOICEDOCTR@AOL.COM
WEBSITE: WWW.VOICE-DOCTOR.COM

June 9, 2005

Mr. Arthur Ochs Sulzberger
Chairman Emeritus
The *New York Times*
229 West 43rd Street
New York, NY 10038

Mr. Sulzberger,

The New York Times editorial page, June 9, 2005 has a blurb about the (White) House party for lobbyists. The editorial says, "The White House censored two Environmental Protection Agency reports that linked warming to industrial activity. It's sad to think of a White House run by people who believe that a problem can be edited out of existence."

It is sad to think of *The New York Times* editing out cures of hopeless voice problems out of existence. Brody's column in 1992 and the front page of *The New York Times* March 2, 2003 edited out cures of Spasmodic Dysphonia (SD) by me. Enclosed is a printout for your review.

Most cordially,

Morton Cooper, Ph.D.

MC/aa
Enclosure

cc: Arthur Sulzberger, Jr.
    Cornelia Dean
    Bill Keller
    Jane E. Brody

Bibliography

Books

Cooper, Morton. *One Lone Courageous Doctor Curing Strangled Voices (SD) Spasmodic Dysphonia vs The New York Times and The Entire Medical Establishment Guaranteeing No Cures, Part 1.* Los Angeles: Voice & Speech Company of America. 2008.

Cooper, Morton. *One Lone Courageous Doctor Curing Strangled Voices (SD) Spasmodic Dysphonia vs The New York Times and The Entire Medical Establishment Guaranteeing No Cures, Part 2.* Los Angeles: Voice & Speech Company of America. 2008.

Cooper, Morton and John Curtis. *Curing Hopeless Voices: The Strangled Voice (Spasmodic Dysphonia) & Other Voice Problems with Direct Voice Rehabilitation.* Los Angeles: Voice & Speech Company of America, 2006.

Cooper, Morton. *The Games We Play With Our Voices.* Los Angeles: Voice & Speech Company of America, 2006.

Cooper, Morton. *Pet Talk.* Los Angeles: Voice & Speech Company of America, 2006.

Cooper, Morton. *Confessions of a Hollywood Voice & Speech Coach.* Los Angeles: Voice & Speech Company of America, 2006.

Cooper, Morton. *Stop Committing Voice Suicide.* 7th printing. Los Angeles: Voice & Speech Company of America, 1996.

Cooper, Morton. *Winning With You Voice.* Hollywood, FL: Frederick Fell Publishers, Inc., 1989. 4th printing. Los Angeles: Voice & Speech Company of America, 1990.

Cooper, Morton. *Change Your Voice, Change Your Life.* New York: Macmillan Publishing Company, 1984. Paperback-New York: Harper Collins, Publishers, 1985. 18th Printing. Los Angeles: Voice & Speech Company of America, 1996.

Cooper, Morton. *Modern Techniques of Voice Rehabilitation.* Springfield, IL: Charles C. Thomas, 1973.

Cooper, Morton and Marcia Cooper (eds.). *Approaches to Vocal Rehabilitation.* Springfield, IL: Charles C. Thomas, 1977.

Chapters

Cooper, Morton. "Treatment of Functional Aphonia and Dysphonia," in Perkins, William (ed.) *Current Therapy of Communication Disorders*. New York: Thieme & Stratton, Inc., 1983.

Cooper, Morton. "Modern Techniques of Vocal Rehabilitation for Functional and Organic Dysphonias," in Travis, L.E (ed.). *Handbook of Speech Pathology and Audiology*. New York: Appleton-Century-Crofts, 1971.

Cooper, Morton. "Management of Voice, Speech, and Language Disorders," in Gellis, S.S. and B.M. Kagan (ed.). *Current Pediatric Therapy*. 9th ed. Philadelphia: W.B. Saunders Company, 1980. (Also 8th ed., 1978; 7th ed., 1976; 6th ed., 1973).

Cooper, Morton. "Speaking Voice of the Singer," in Hines, Jerome. *Great Singers On Great Singing*. New York: Doubleday & Company, 1982.

Audio Digest

Cooper, Morton. "Techniques of Vocal Rehabilitation for Functional and Organic Voice Disorders," in Bradford, Larry and Robert Wertz (eds.). *Communicative Disorder: an Audio Journal for Continuing Education*, 4 (March 1979), Grune and Stratton, Inc.

Articles

Cooper, Morton. "Doctors' Dialogue: Untold Story of President Clinton's Hoarse Voice," *Lets Live* (September 1994), 88.

Cooper, Morton. "The Miracle Voice and Speech Doctor," *Lets Live* (February 1994), 72-73.

Cooper, Morton. "The Voice That Came In From The Cold," *Lets Live* (January 1994), 28-30.

Cooper, Morton. "Treating Laryngitis with Voice Therapy," *Advance* (January 10, 1994), 9.

Cooper, Morton. "Who Killed Voices?" *Lets Live* (August 1993), 24-26.

Cooper, Morton. "Treating Spasmodic Dysphonia with Direct Voice Rehabilitation," *Advance* (February 1, 1993), 6-7.

Cooper, Morton. "Don't Put Up With Voice Fatigue," *Wall Street Journal* (September 28, 1992), A-14.

Cooper, Morton. "Change Your Voice, Change Your Life," *Cosmopolitan* (July 1984), 138-142.

Cooper, Morton. "Prescriptions for Vocal Health: Finding the Right Vocal Register," *Music Educators Journal*, 69 (February 1983), 40, 57, 59, 61.

Cooper, Morton. "Perceptions for Vocal Health: Medication and the Voice," *Music Educators Journal*, 69 (February 1983), 41-42.

Cooper, Morton. "The Tired Speaking Voice and the Negative Effect on the Singing Voice," *The Nats Bulletin*, 39 (November/December 1982), 11-13.

Cooper, Morton. "A Case History: Stevie Nicks," *Voice*, 4 (September/October 1980), 34.

Cooper, Morton. "Vocal Image and Vocal Identity," *Voice*, 3 (July/August 1980), 36.

Cooper, Morton. "Facts and Fantasies About the Speaking Voice and the Effect Upon the Singing Voice," *Voice*, 2 (May/June 1980), 34.

Cooper, Morton. "The Speaking Voice of the Singer," *Voice*, 1 (March/April 1980), 8-11.

Cooper, Morton. "The Strangled Voice," *Lets Live*, 48 (January 1980), 71-76.

Cooper, Morton. "Aphasia--When the Words Don't Come Out Right," *Lets Live*, 4 (Sept. 1979), 90, 93, 94, 96.

Cooper, Morton. "The Impressive Voice in the Court," *Trial*, 15 (July 1979), 53-55, 69.

Cooper, Morton. "The Voice Problems of Stutterers: A Practical Approach from Clinical Experience," *Journal of Fluency Disorders*, 4 (June 1979), 141-148.

Cooper, Morton. "Be Good to Your Voice," *Prevention*, 31 (May 1979), 142-147.

Cooper, Morton. "The Secret Stutterers," *Lets Live*, 47 (May 1979).

Cooper, Morton. "The Speaking Voice and the Trial Lawyer," *Advocate*, 6 (December 1978), 11-13.

Cooper, Morton. "Spectrographic Analysis of Fundamental Frequency and Hoarseness Before and After Vocal Rehabilitation," *Journal of Speech and Hearing Disorders*, 39 (August 1974), 286-297.

Cooper, Morton. "Prevailing Voice Disorders," *United Teacher*, 4 (September 1972), 13.

Cooper, Morton. "The Stage Voice," *Equity*, LVII (March 1972), 21-22.

Cooper, Morton. "Speech Disorders and Problems," (Aphasia), Pediatric News, 6 (January 1972), 21.

Cooper, Morton. "Speech Voice and Problems," (Stuttering), *Pediatric News*, 5 (November 1971), 55-56.

Cooper, Morton. "The Vocal Image and Voice Suicide," *Voices: The Art and Science of Psychotherapy, Special Issue: Unspoken Behavior*, 6 (August 1971), 26-28.

Cooper, Morton. "Speech Disorders and Problems" (Voice Disorders), *Pediatric News*, 5 (March 1971) 48-49.

Cooper, Morton. "Papillomata of the Vocal Folds: I. Review of the Literature, II. A Program of Vocal Rehabilitation," *Journal of Speech and Hearing Disorders*, 36 (February 1971), 51-60.

Cooper, Morton. "Rehabilitation of Paralytic Dysphonia," *Eye, Ear, Nose and Throat Monthly*, 49 (December 1, 1970), 532-535.

Cooper, Morton. "Vocal Suicide in Newscasters and Announcers - The 'Impressive' Voice," *Radio-Television News Directors Association Bulletin* (December 1970), 21.

Cooper, Morton. "Stopping Vocal Suicide Among Preachers," *Christian Advocate* (December 1970), 11-12.

Cooper, Morton. "Voice Therapy for Teachers," *Education*, 91 (November/December 1970), 142-146.

Cooper, Morton. "A Broadcaster's Artistic Voice," *The Quill*, 58 (October 1970), 19.

Cooper, Morton. "Vocal Suicide Among Rabbis," *Central Conference of American Rabbis Journal*, 17 (October 1970), 70-73.

Cooper, Morton. "Vocal Suicide of the Speaking Voice in Singers," *Music Educators Journal*, 59 (September 1970), 53-54.

Cooper, Morton. "Vocal Suicide Among Theologians," *Your Church*, 3 (July/August 1970), 16-21.

Cooper, Morton. "Voice Problems of the Geriatric Patient," *Geriatrics*, 25 (June 1970), 107-110.

Cooper, Morton. "Voice Suicide in Teachers," *Peabody Journal of Education*, 47 (May 1970), 334-337.

Cooper, Morton. "Speech Disorders and Problems," (Part I), *Pediatric News*, 4 (March 1970), 16, 37.

Cooper Morton. " Speech Disorders and Problems," (Part II), *Pediatric News*, 4 (April 1970), 27, 57.

Cooper, Morton. "Speech Disorders and Problems," (Part III), *Pediatric News*, 4 (May 1970), 27, 48.

Cooper, Morton, "Teacher, Save That Voice!" *Grade Teacher*, 87 (March 1970), 71-72, 74, 76.

Cooper, Morton . "Vocal Suicide in Singers," *The Nats Bulletin*, 26 (February/March 1970), 7-10, 31.

Cooper, Morton. "Vocal Rehabilitation-Current Opinion," *Medical Tribune*, 11 (February 23, 1970), 11.

Cooper, Morton. "Vocal Suicide in the Legal Profession," *Bar Bulletin*, 43 (1968), 453-456. Reprinted in *Case and Comment*, 75 (January/February 1970), 44-47.

Cooper, Morton. "Rehabilitation of Paralytic Dysphonia," *California Medicine*, 112 (February 1970), 18-20.

Cooper, Morton. "Vocal Suicide in the Theatrical Profession," *The Screen Actor*, 11 (November/December 1969), 8-9.

Cooper, Morton. "In Consultation," *Medical Tribune*, 10 (August 28, 1969), 13.

Cooper, Morton and Yanagihara, Naoaki. "A Study of Basal Pitch Level Variations Found in the Normal Speaking Voice of Males and Females," *Journal of Communication Disorders*, 3 (1971), 261-266.

Cooper, Morton and Nahum, Alan M. "Vocal Rehabilitation for Contact Ulcer of the Larynx," *Archives of Otolaryngology*, 85 (1967), 41-46.

Satou, Alan and Cooper, Morton. "Psychiatric Observations of Falsetto Voice," *The Voice*, 17 (February 1968), 31-33, 35, 37, 39, 41.

Column

Voice Disorders: Questions and Answers with Dr. Cooper, *United Teacher*, 1973-1975.

Presentations

Cooper, Morton. Extended Seminar: "Spasmodic Dysphonia: Cures, Recoveries and Improvement by Direct Voice Rehabilitation," *American Speech-Language-Hearing Association Annual Convention*, 2000.

Cooper, Morton. "Presenting Cures, Recoveries and Improvements by DVR.," *XIth Annual Pacific Voice Conference*, November 5-7, 1998.

Cooper, Morton. "Recovery from Spastic Dysphonia by Direct Voice Rehabilitation," *Proceeding from the 18th Congress of the International Association of Logopedics and Phoniatrics*, 1 (August 1980), 579-584.

Cooper, Morton. Mini-seminar: "Recovery from Spastic Dysphonia by Direct Voice Rehabilitation" and Mini-seminar "Direct Vocal Training of the Speaking Voice for Speech Clinicians," *California Speech-Language-Hearing Association Annual Conference*, 1980.

Cooper, Morton. Mini-seminar: "Techniques of Vocal Rehabilitation for Functional and Organic Dysphonias" and mini-seminar: "Considerations for the Treatment of Voice Disorders," *American Speech-Language-Hearing Association Annual Convention*, 1979.

Cooper, Morton. Mini-seminar: "What Vocal Rehabilitation is all About," *California Speech-Language-Hearing Association Annual Conference*, 1978.

Cooper, Morton. "Vocal Rehabilitation for Spastic Dysphonia and Incipient Spastic Dysphonia," *American Speech-Language-Hearing Association Annual Convention*, 1974.

Cooper, Morton. "Vocal Rehabilitation for Spastic Dysphonia and Incipient Spastic Dysphonia" and Mini-short Course: "Voice Training for Speech Therapists," *California Speech-Language-Hearing Association Annual Conference*, 1973.

Cooper, Morton. "Vocal Rehabilitation for Pre-malignant Growths of Vocal Folds," *American Speech-Language-Hearing Association Annual Convention*, 1972.

Cooper, Morton. "Vocal Suicide and Vocal Rehabilitation" and "What Can Be Done for Spastic Dysphonia?" *California Speech-Language-Hearing Association Annual Conference*, 1970.